# *Taylor Swift* FEARLESS

ISBN 978-1-4234-8164-5

HAL•LEONARD®
CORPORATION

7777 W. BLUEMOUND RD. P.O. BOX 13819 MILWAUKEE, WI 53213

Visit Hal Leonard Online at
**www.halleonard.com**

# STRUM AND PICK PATTERNS

This chart contains the suggested strum and pick patterns that are referred to by number at the beginning of each song in this book. The symbols ⊓ and ∨ in the strum patterns refer to down and up strokes, respectively. The letters in the pick patterns indicate which right-hand fingers plays which strings.

p = thumb
i = index finger
m = middle finger
a = ring finger

For example; Pick Pattern 2
is played: thumb - index - middle - ring

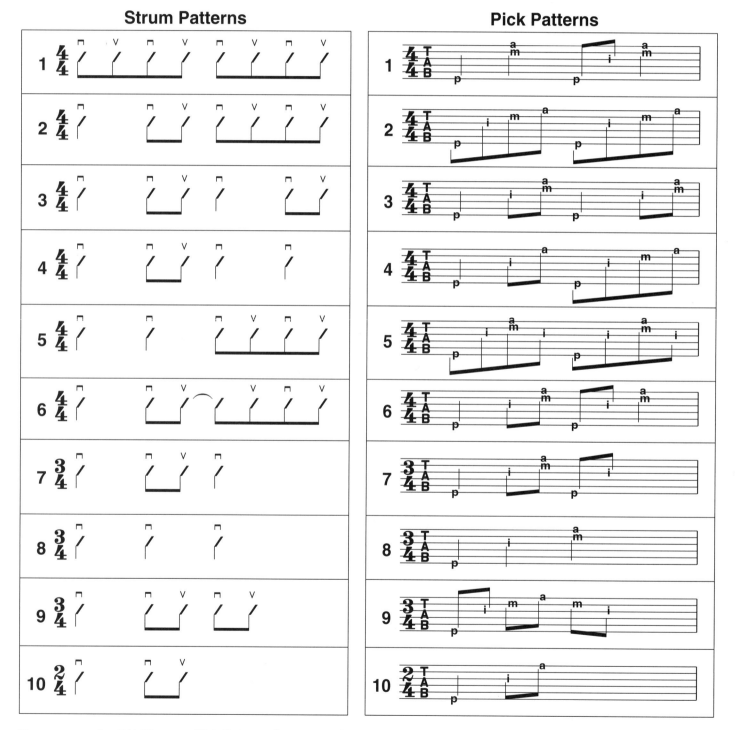

You can use the 3/4 Strum or Pick Patterns in songs written in compound meter (6/8, 9/8, 12/8, etc.).
For example, you can accompany a song in 6/8 by playing the 3/4 pattern twice in each measure.
The 4/4 Strum and Pick Patterns can be used for songs written in cut time (¢) by doubling the note time values in the patterns. Each pattern would therefore last two measures in cut time.

# Fearless

**Words and Music by Taylor Swift, Liz Rose and Hillary Lindsey**

*Capo III

**Strum Pattern: 2, 4**
**Pick Pattern: 6**

Intro
Moderately

*Optional: To match recording, place capo at 3rd fret.

1. There's some-thin' 'bout the way the street looks when it's just rained. There's a glow off the pave-ment. You walk me to the

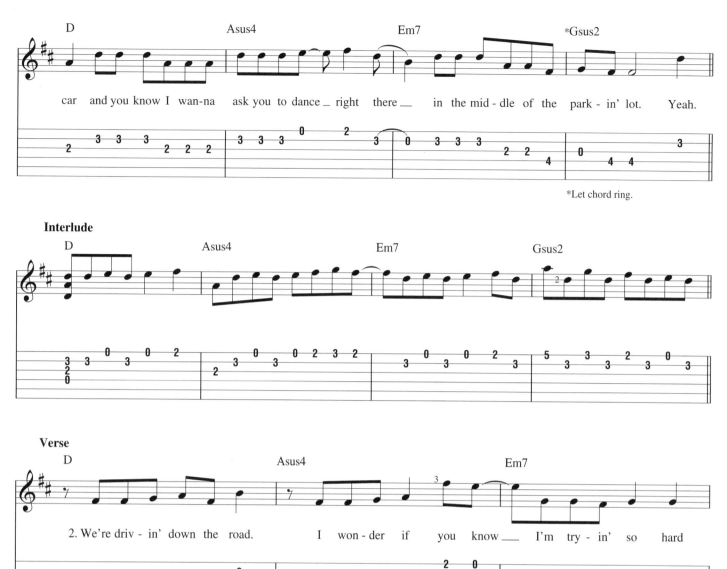

*Let chord ring.

**Interlude**

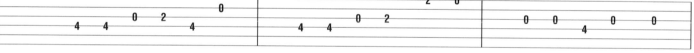

**Verse**

**𝄋 Chorus**

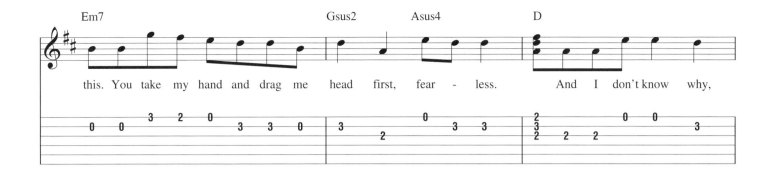

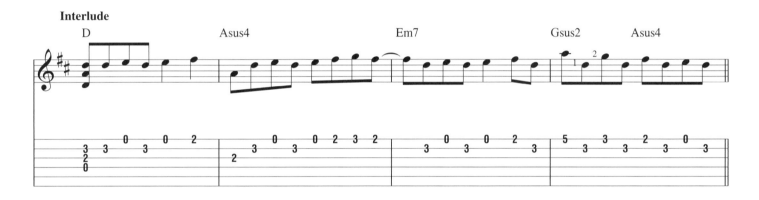

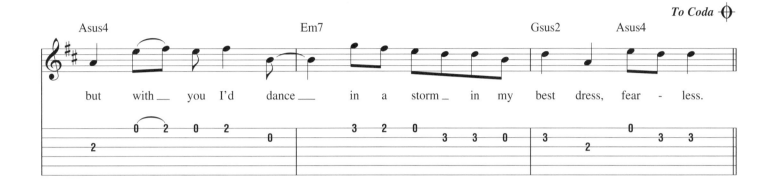

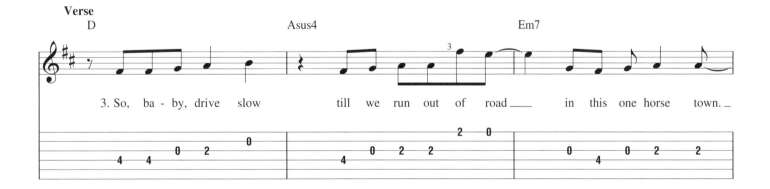

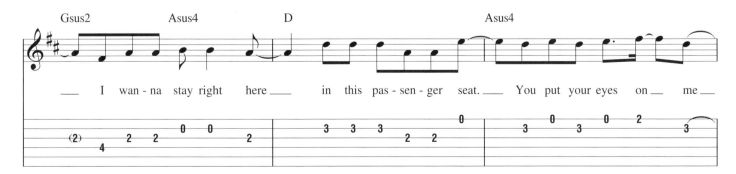

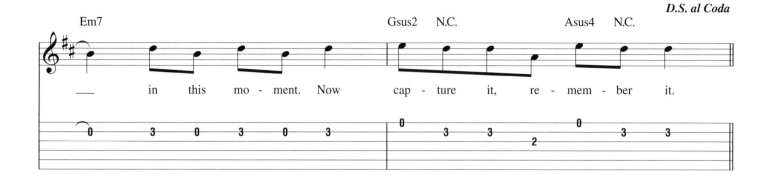

in this mo - ment. Now cap - ture it, re - mem - ber it.

### ⊕ Coda
**Guitar Solo**

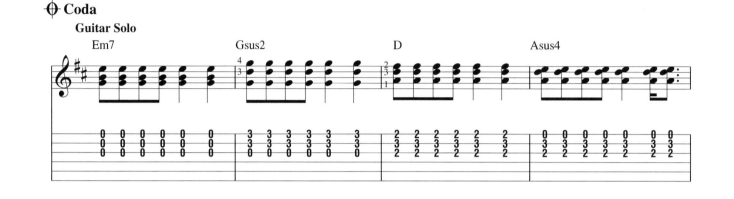

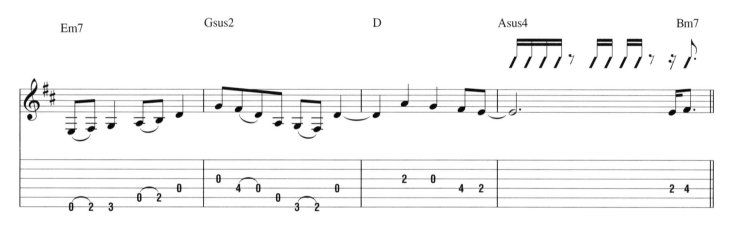

**Bridge**

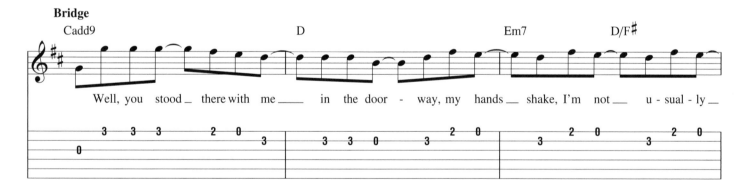

Well, you stood __ there with me ____ in the door - way, my hands __ shake, I'm not __ u - sual - ly __

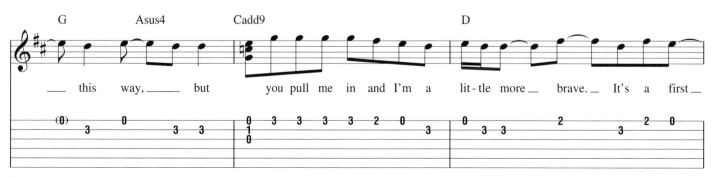

__ this way, ____ but you pull me in and I'm a lit - tle more __ brave. __ It's a first __

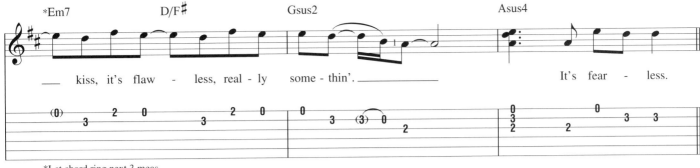

**Interlude**

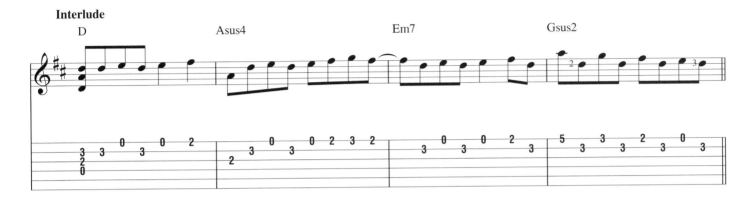

**Chorus**

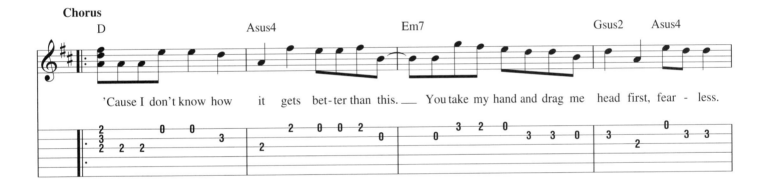

**Outro**

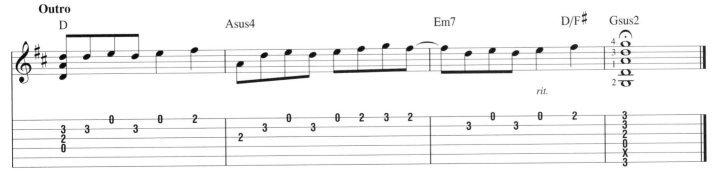

7

# Fifteen

**Words and Music by Taylor Swift**

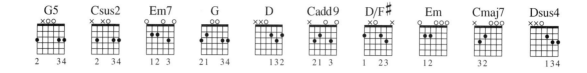

**Strum Pattern: 3, 6**
**Pick Pattern: 2, 5**

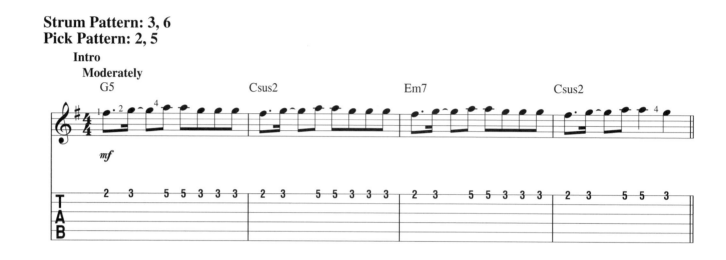

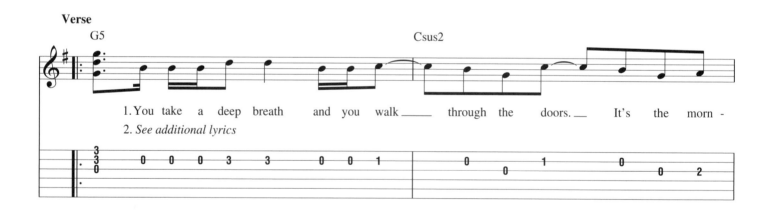

*2nd time, let chord ring.

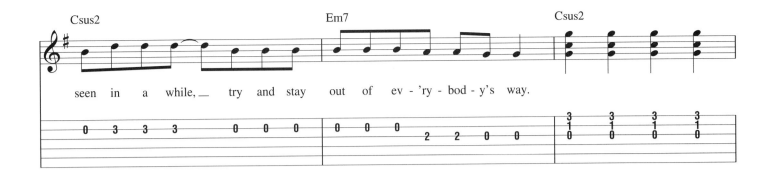

seen in a while, __ try and stay out of ev - 'ry - bod - y's way.

It's your fresh - man year and you're gon - na be here __ for the next four years in this

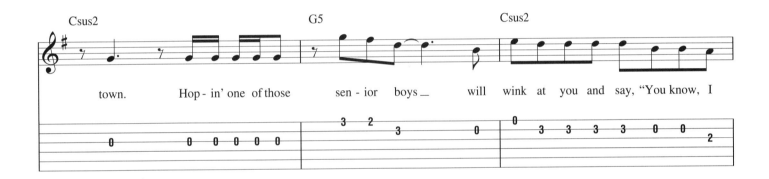

town. Hop - in' one of those sen - ior boys __ will wink at you and say, "You know, I

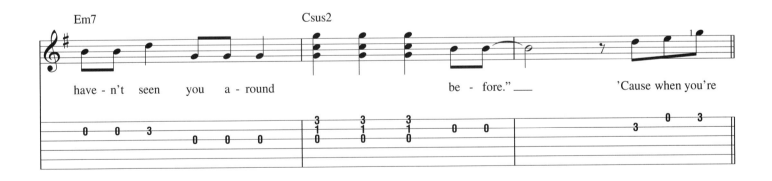

have - n't seen you a - round be - fore." __ 'Cause when you're

**Chorus**

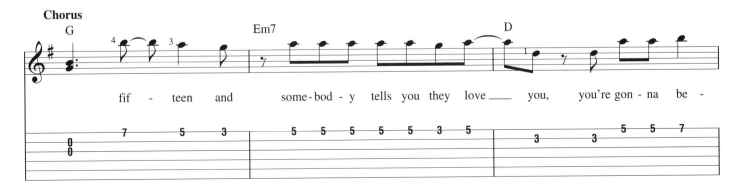

fif - teen and some-bod - y tells you they love __ you, you're gon - na be -

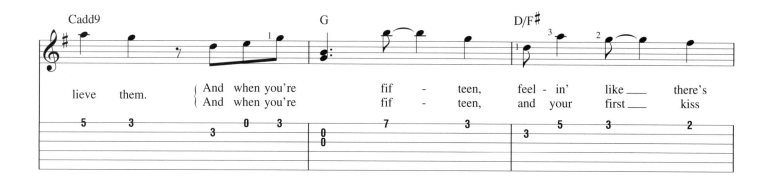

Cadd9      G      D/F#

lieve them. { And when you're fif - teen, feel - in' like ___ there's
{ And when you're fif - teen, and your first ___ kiss

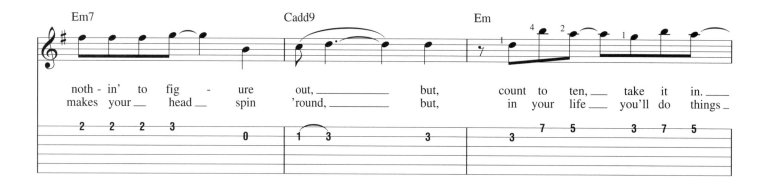

Em7      Cadd9      Em

noth - in' to fig - ure out, _____ but, count to ten, ___ take it in. ___
makes your ___ head ___ spin 'round, _____ but, in your life ___ you'll do things ___

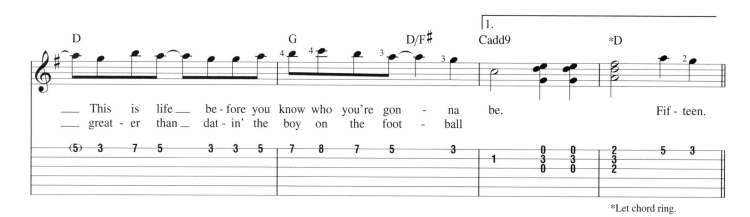

D      G    D/F#    Cadd9      *D

1.

___ This is life ___ be - fore you know who you're gon - na be. Fif - teen.
___ great - er than ___ dat - in' the boy on the foot - ball

*Let chord ring.

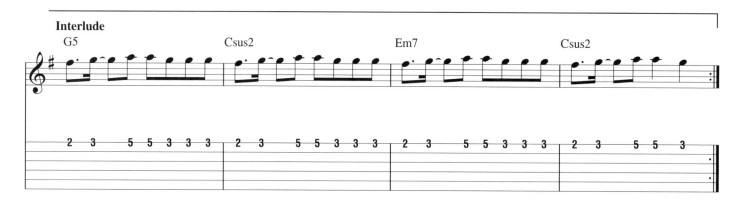

**Interlude**

G5      Csus2      Em7      Csus2

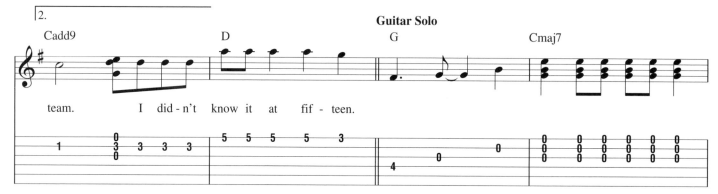

2.

**Guitar Solo**

Cadd9      D      G      Cmaj7

team. I did - n't know it at fif - teen.

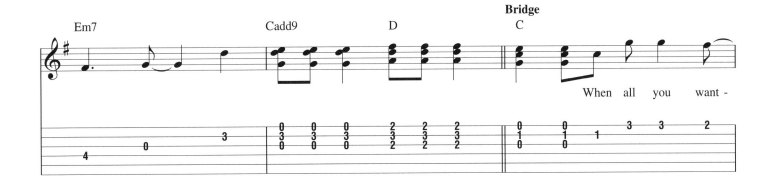

**Bridge**

When all you want -

- ed was to be want - ed, wish you could go back and tell your-self what you know now.

**Verse**

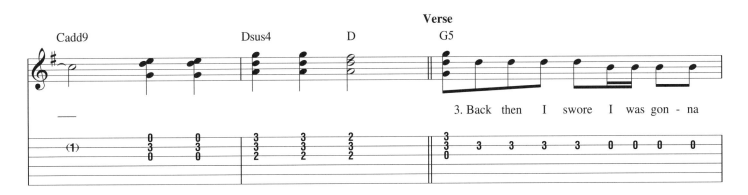

3. Back then I swore I was gon - na

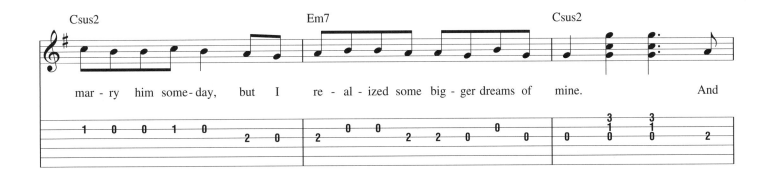

mar - ry him some - day, but I re - al - ized some big - ger dreams of mine. And

Ab - i - gail gave ev - 'ry - thing she had to a boy who changed his mind.

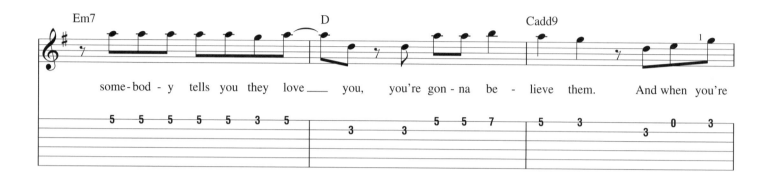

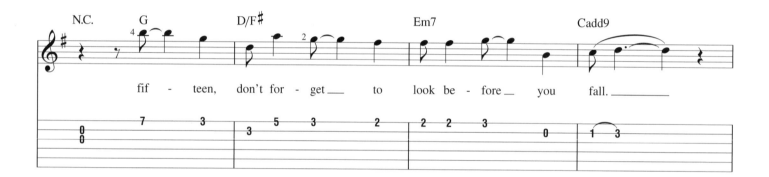

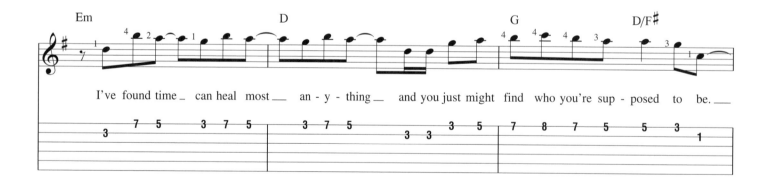

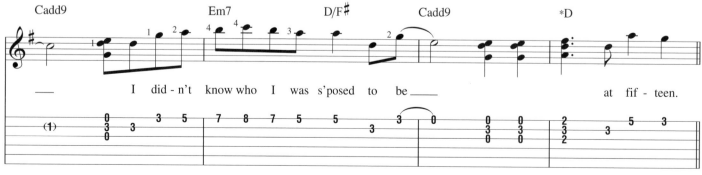

*Let chord ring.

**Outro**

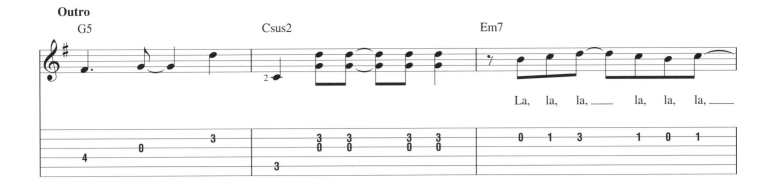

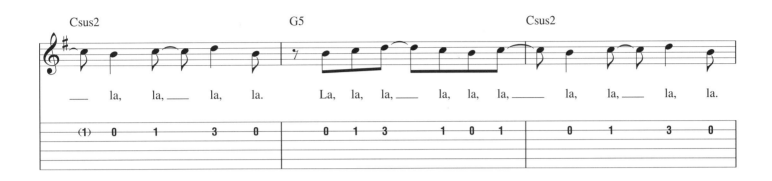

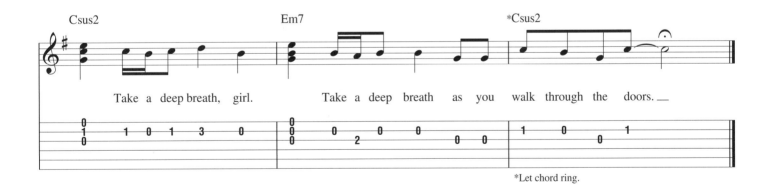

*Let chord ring.

*Additional Lyrics*

2. You sit in class next to a redhead named Abigail
   And soon enough we're best friends,
   Laughin' at the other girls who think they're so cool.
   We'll be out of here as soon as we can.
   And then you're on your very first date
   And he's got a car and you're feelin' like flyin'.
   And you mama's waitin' up and you're thinkin' he's the one
   And you're dancin' 'round your room when the night ends,
   When the night ends.

# Love Story

**Words and Music by Taylor Swift**

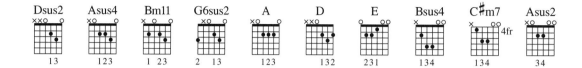

**Strum Pattern: 1, 6**
**Pick Pattern: 4**

Intro

Moderately

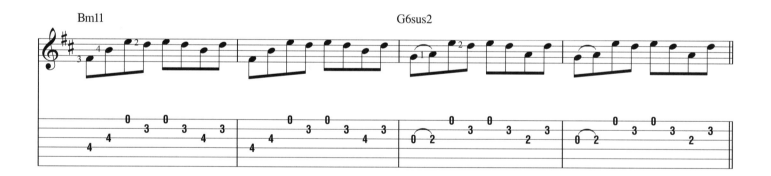

**Verse**

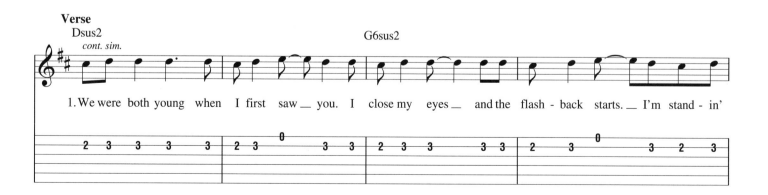

1. We were both young when I first saw __ you. I close my eyes __ and the flash - back starts. __ I'm stand - in'

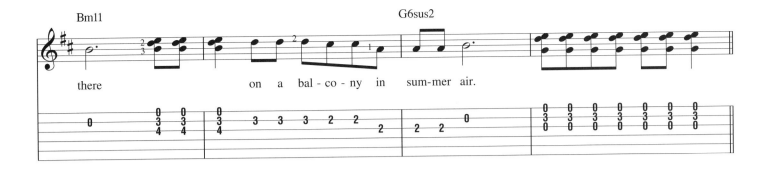

there on a bal-co-ny in sum-mer air.

**Verse**

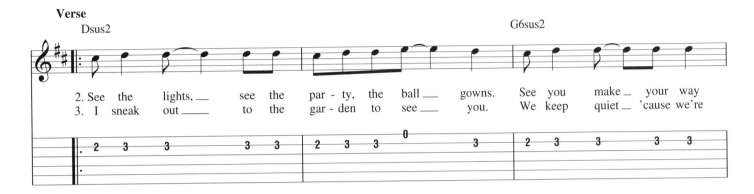

2. See the lights, __ see the par - ty, the ball __ gowns. See you make __ your way
3. I sneak out ____ to the gar - den to see __ you. We keep quiet __ 'cause we're

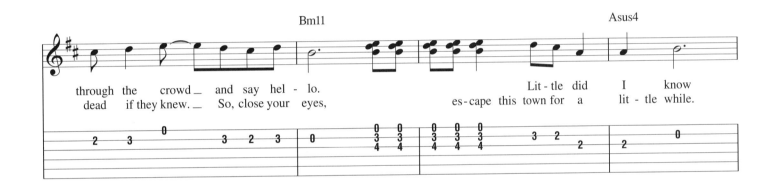

through the crowd __ and say hel - lo. Lit - tle did I know
dead if they knew. __ So, close your eyes, es - cape this town for a lit - tle while.

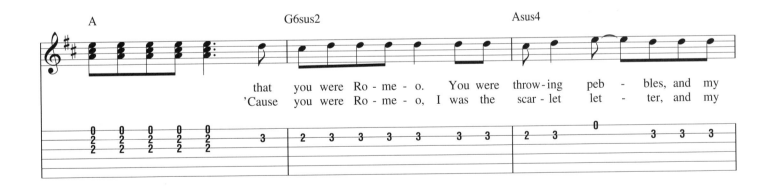

that you were Ro - me - o. You were throw-ing peb - bles, and my
'Cause you were Ro - me - o, I was the scar - let let - ter, and my

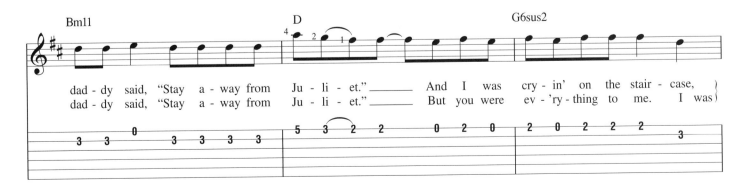

dad - dy said, "Stay a - way from Ju - li - et." ____ And I was cry - in' on the stair - case,
dad - dy said, "Stay a - way from Ju - li - et." ____ But you were ev - 'ry-thing to me. I was

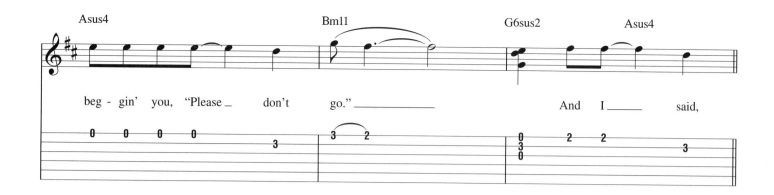

beg - gin' you, "Please _ don't go." _____ And I _____ said,

**Chorus**

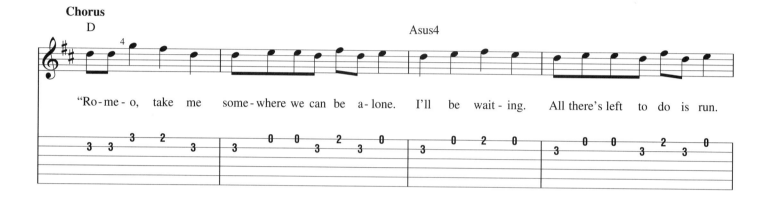

"Ro - me - o, take me some - where we can be a - lone. I'll be wait - ing. All there's left to do is run.

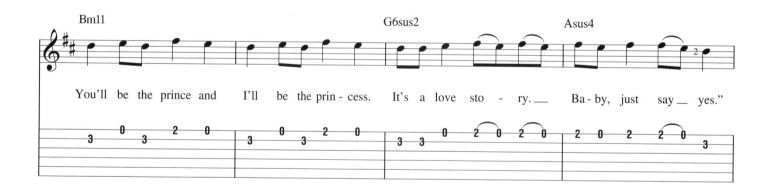

You'll be the prince and I'll be the prin - cess. It's a love sto - ry. _ Ba - by, just say _ yes."

3. So, "Ro - me - o, save me. They're try'n' to tell me how to feel.

This love is dif - fi - cult, but it's __ real. __ Don't be a - fraid. We'll make it out of this mess.

**Interlude**

It's a love sto - ry. __ Ba - by, just say __ yes."

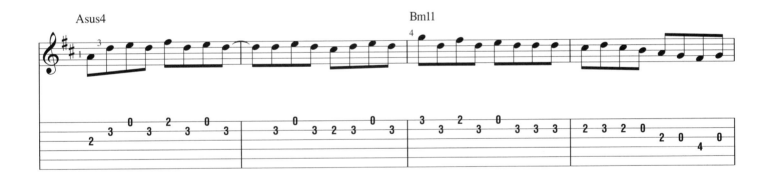

**Bridge**

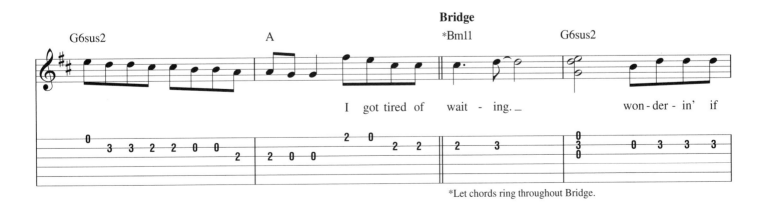

I got tired of wait - ing. __ won - der - in' if

\*Let chords ring throughout Bridge.

you were ev - er com-ing a - round. My faith in you was fad - ing when I

**Chorus**

met you on the out - skirts of town. And I said, "Ro-me - o, save me. I've been feel - in' so a - lone.

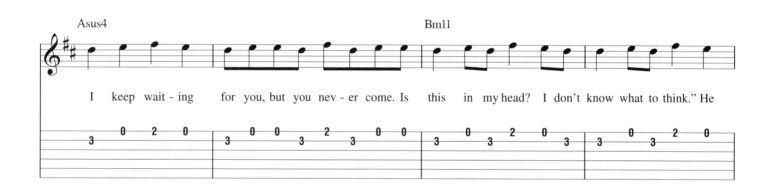

I keep wait - ing for you, but you nev - er come. Is this in my head? I don't know what to think." He

knelt to the ground and pulled out a ring and said, "Mar-ry me, Ju - li - et, you nev-er have to be a - lone.

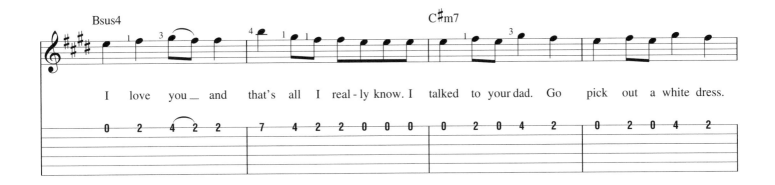

I love you __ and that's all I real - ly know. I talked to your dad. Go pick out a white dress.

**Outro**

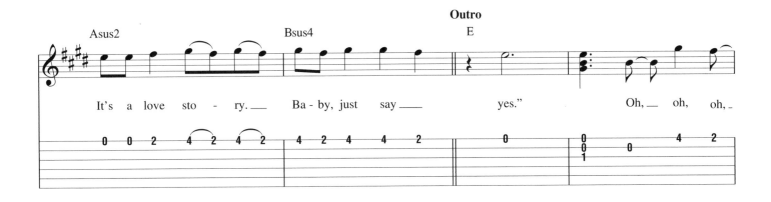

It's a love sto - ry. __ Ba - by, just say __ yes." Oh, __ oh, oh, _

__ oh, __ oh, oh, __ oh. 'Cause

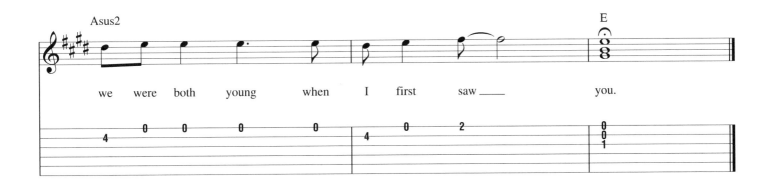

we were both young when I first saw __ you.

# Hey Stephen

**Words and Music by Taylor Swift**

*Tune down 1/2 step:
(low to high) E♭-A♭-D♭-G♭-B♭-E♭

## Strum Pattern: 4, 6
## Pick Pattern: 4, 6

**Intro**

**Moderately**

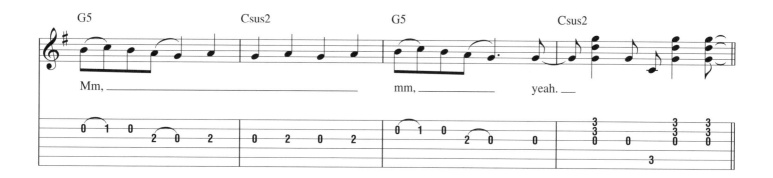

*Optional: To match recording, tune down 1/2 step.

**Verse**

1. Hey, Stephen, I know looks can be de-ceiv-in', but I know I saw a light in you.
2. *See additional lyrics*

**Omit ties 2nd time

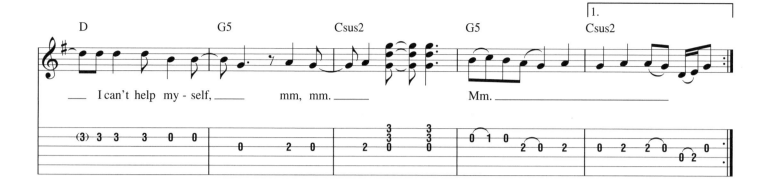

I can't help my-self, _____ mm, mm. _____ Mm. _____

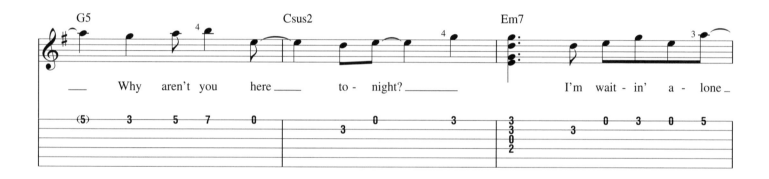

**Bridge**

They're dim-min' the street _____ lights, you're per-fect for me. _____ Why aren't you here _____ to-night? _____ I'm wait-in' a-lone _____

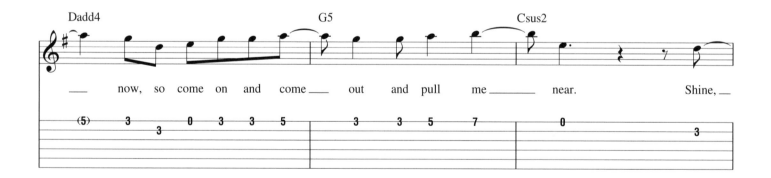

now, so come on and come _____ out and pull me _____ near. Shine, _____

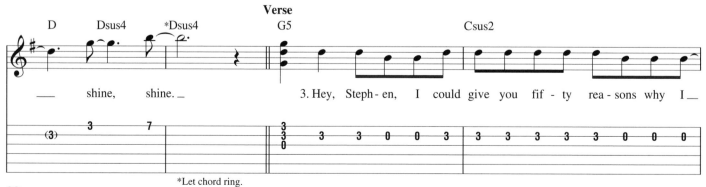

**Verse**

_____ shine, shine. _____ 3. Hey, Steph-en, I could give you fif-ty rea-sons why I _____

*Let chord ring.

_____ should be the one you choose. All those oth - er girls,

*D.S. al Coda*

we'll they're beau - ti - ful, but would they write a song for you?

$\oplus$ **Coda**

**Chorus**

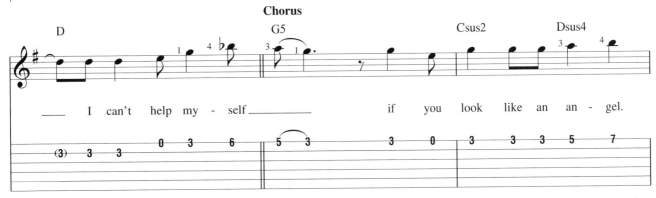

_____ I can't help my - self _____ if you look like an an - gel.

Can't help it if I wan - na kiss you in the rain. So, come feel this mag - ic I've been

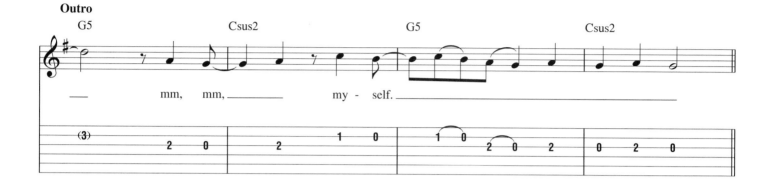

**Outro**

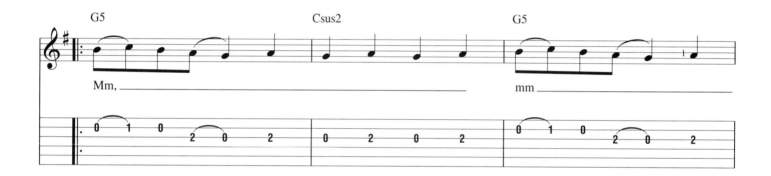

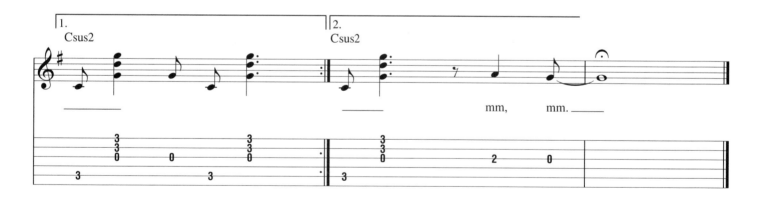

*Additional Lyrics*

2. Hey, Stephen, I've been holdin' back this feelin',
So I've got some things to say to you.
I seen it all, so I thought, but I never
Seen nobody shine the way you do.
The way you walk, way you talk, way you say my name,
It's beautiful, wonderful, don't you ever change.
Hey, Stephen, why are people always leavin'?
I think you and I should stay the same.

# White Horse

**Words and Music by Taylor Swift and Liz Rose**

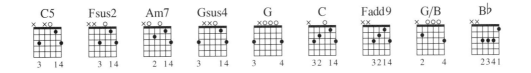

**Strum Pattern: 3, 6**
**Pick Pattern: 2, 5**

Intro
Moderately

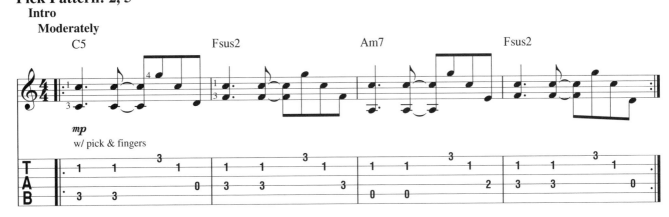

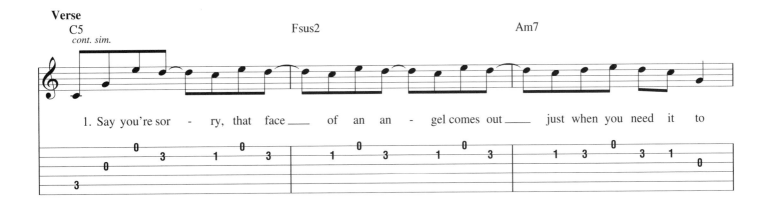

1. Say you're sor - ry, that face of an an - gel comes out just when you need it to

as I paced back and forth all this time 'cause I

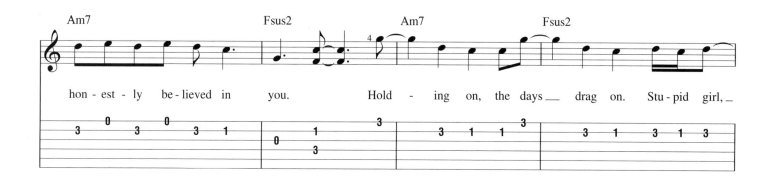

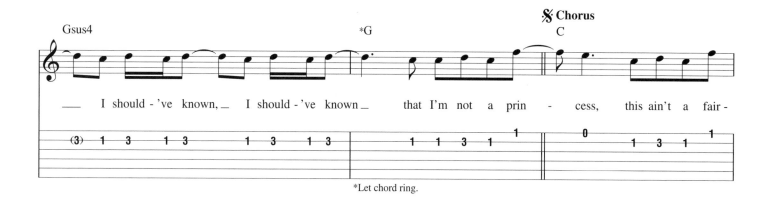

*Let chord ring.

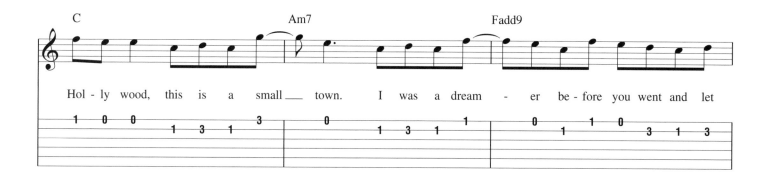

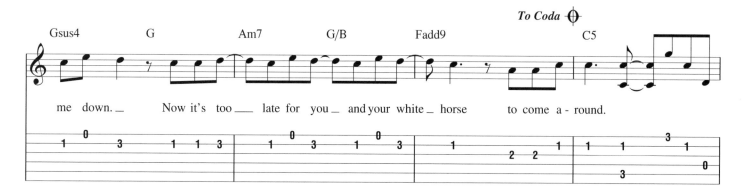

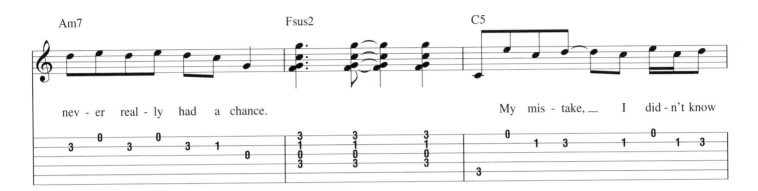

*Let chord ring.

**Bridge**

And there you are on your knees, beg - gin' for for - give - ness,

beg - gin' for me, just like I al - ways want - ed, but I'm so ____ sor -

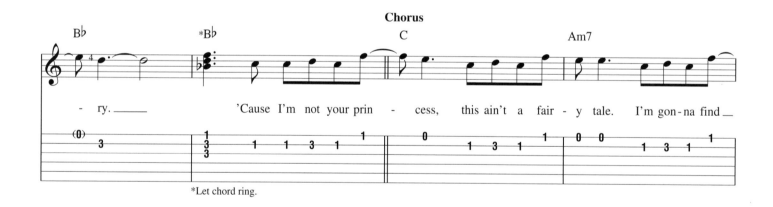

**Chorus**

- ry. ____ 'Cause I'm not your prin - cess, this ain't a fair - y tale. I'm gon-na find ____

*Let chord ring.

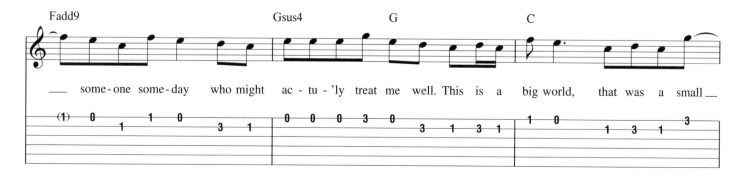

____ some - one some - day who might ac - tu - 'ly treat me well. This is a big world, that was a small ____

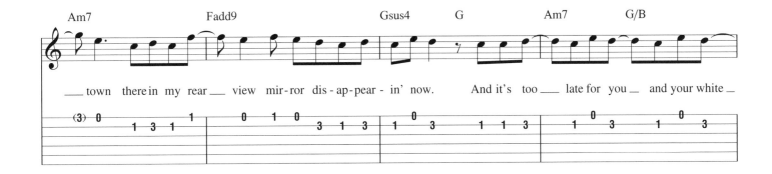

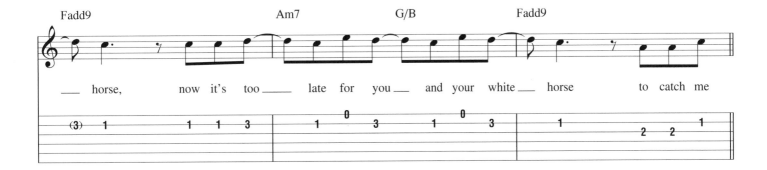

**Outro**

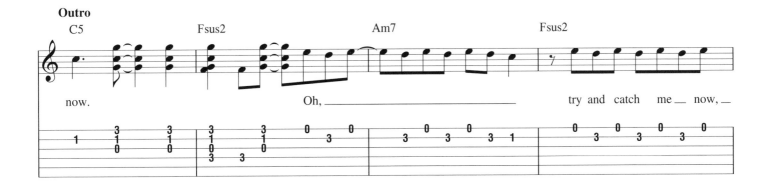

*Let chord ring.

# You Belong with Me

*Words and Music by Taylor Swift and Liz Rose*

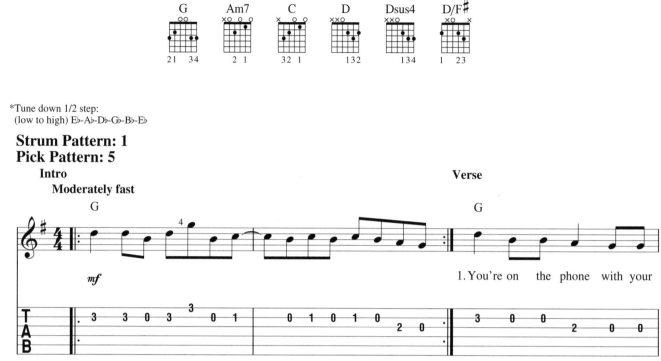

\*Tune down 1/2 step:
(low to high) Eb-Ab-Db-Gb-Bb-Eb

**Strum Pattern: 1**
**Pick Pattern: 5**

Intro
Moderately fast

Verse

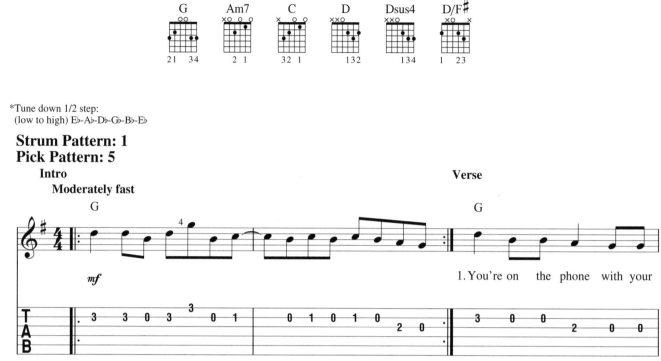

1. You're on the phone with your

\*Optional: To match recording, tune down 1/2 step.

girl - friend. She's up - set. ___ She's go - in' off a - bout some - thin' that ___ you

said. 'Cause she does - n't get your hu - mor like I do.

I'm in the room, it's a typ-i-cal Tues-day night. __ I'm list'-nin' to the kind of mu-sic she does-n't like. __

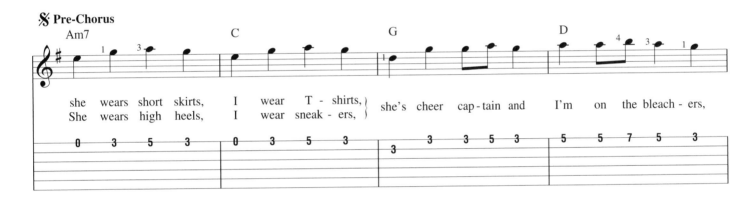

__ And she'll nev-er know your sto-ry like I do. But

**𝄋 Pre-Chorus**

she wears short skirts, I wear T-shirts,  } she's cheer cap-tain and I'm on the bleach-ers,
She wears high heels, I wear sneak-ers,  }

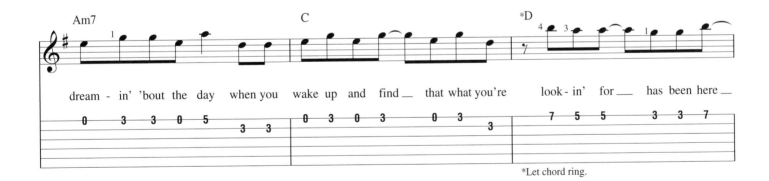

dream-in' 'bout the day when you wake up and find __ that what you're look-in' for __ has been here __

*Let chord ring.

**Chorus**

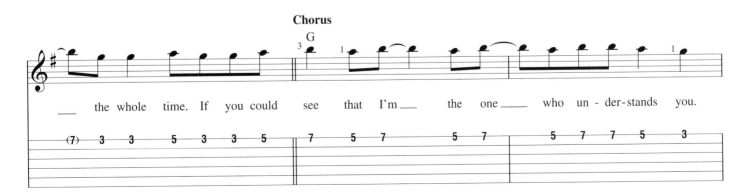

__ the whole time. If you could see that I'm __ the one __ who un-der-stands you.

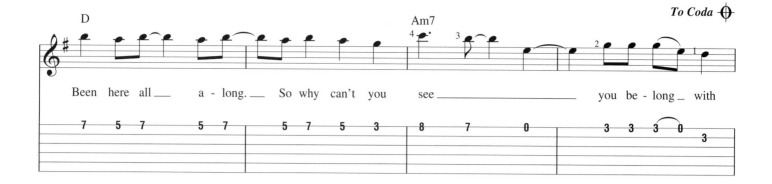

Been here all ___ a - long. ___ So why can't you see _____ you be - long ___ with

me? _____ You be - long ___ with me. ___

*Let chord ring.

**Verse**

2. Walk - in' the streets with you ___ in your worn - out jeans, ___ I can't help think - in' this is

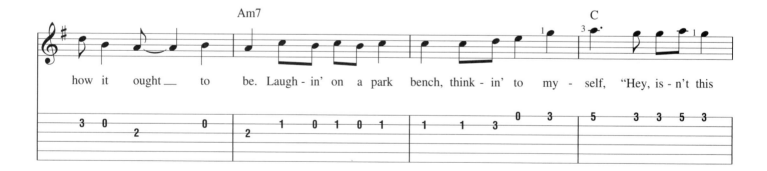

how it ought ___ to be. Laugh - in' on a park bench, think - in' to my - self, "Hey, is - n't this

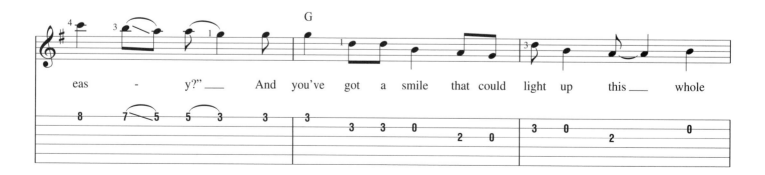

eas - y?" ___ And you've got a smile that could light up this ___ whole

town. I have-n't seen it in a while since she brought you down. __ You say you're fine. I know you

*D.S. al Coda*

bet - ter than that. Hey, what you do - in' with a girl like that?

**⊕ Coda**

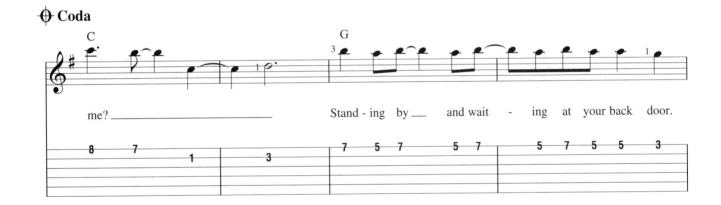

me? _____ Stand - ing by __ and wait - ing at your back door.

All this time __ how could __ you not know, ba - by, _____

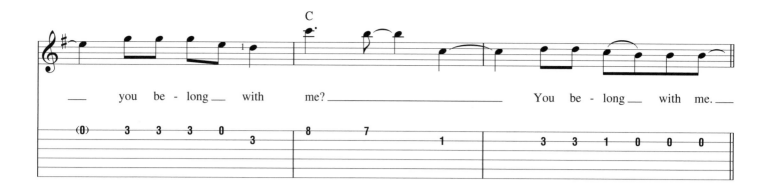

you be - long ___ with me? _____ You be - long ___ with me. ___

**Interlude**

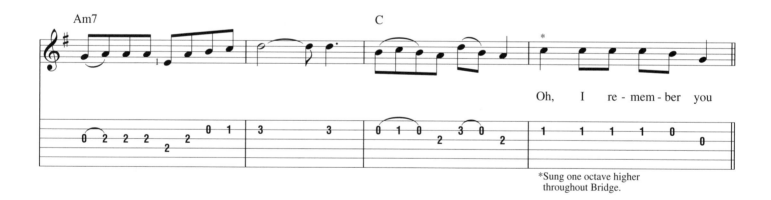

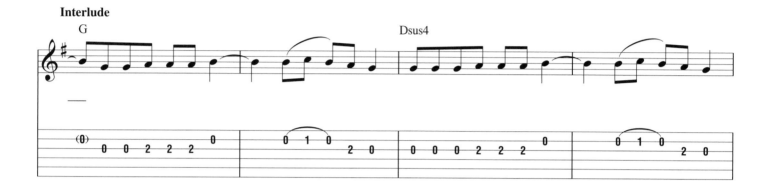

Oh, I re - mem - ber you

*Sung one octave higher
throughout Bridge.

**Bridge**

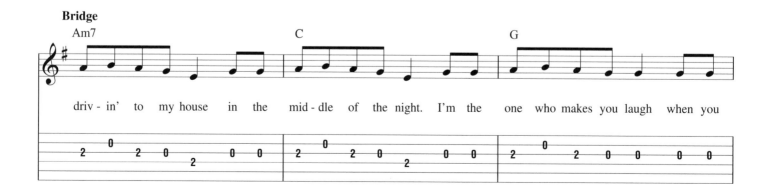

driv - in' to my house in the mid - dle of the night. I'm the one who makes you laugh when you

know you're 'bout to cry. I know your fav-'rite songs and you tell me 'bout your dreams. Think I

know where you be - long. Think I know it's with me. _____ Can't you

*Let chord ring.                                                    **Sung as written.

**Outro-Chorus**

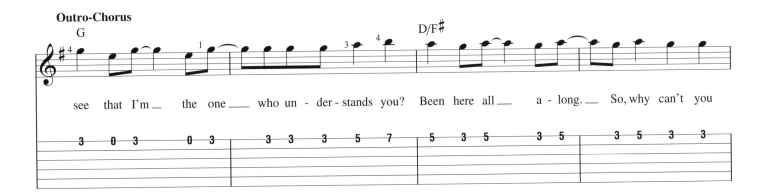

see that I'm ___ the one ___ who un - der - stands you? Been here all ___ a - long. ___ So, why can't you

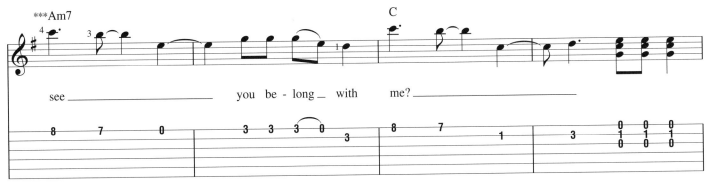

see _____ you be - long ___ with me? _____

***Let chord ring.

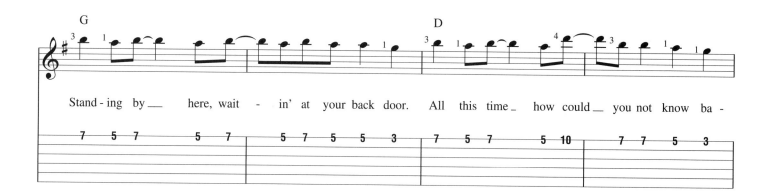

Stand - ing by \_\_ here, wait - in' at your back door. All this time \_ how could \_ you not know ba -

by, _____ you be - long \_ with me? _____ You be - long \_ with me. \_\_

**Outro**

\_\_ You be - long \_ with me. _____ Have you ev - er thought just may -

be _____ you be - long \_ with me? _____ You be - long \_ with me. \_\_

# Breathe

**Words and Music by Taylor Swift and Colbie Caillat**

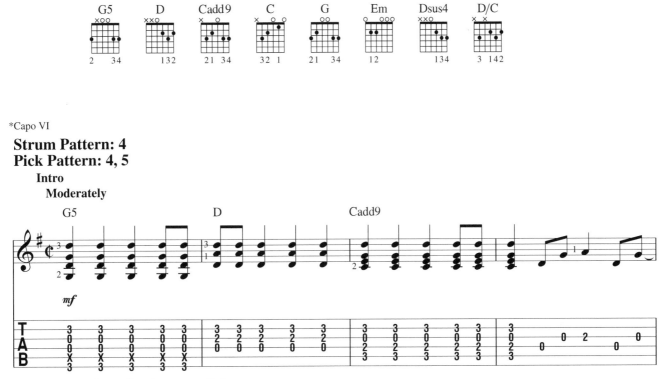

*Capo VI

**Strum Pattern: 4**
**Pick Pattern: 4, 5**

Intro
Moderately

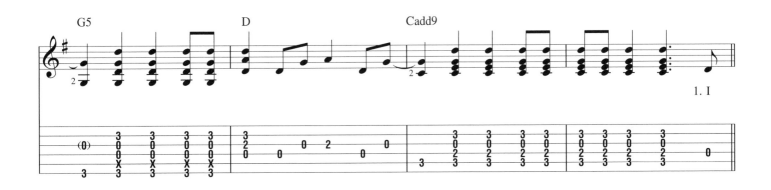

*Optional: To match recording, place capo at 6th fret.

Verse

see   your   face   in my   mind   as   I   drive   a-way___                    'cause

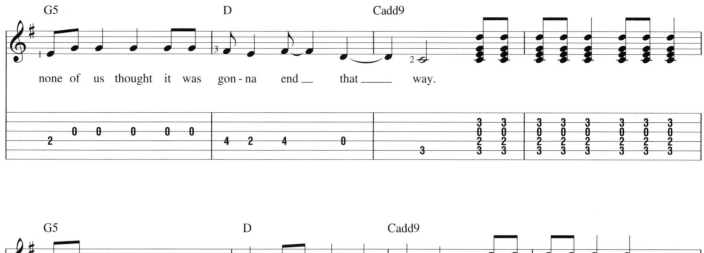

none of us thought it was gon-na end ___ that ___ way.

Peo-ple are peo-ple and some-times we change ___ our ___ minds. But it's

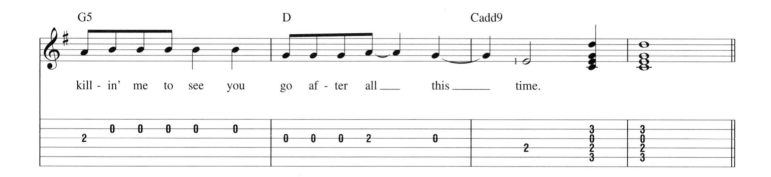

kill-in' me to see you go af-ter all ___ this ___ time.

**Interlude**

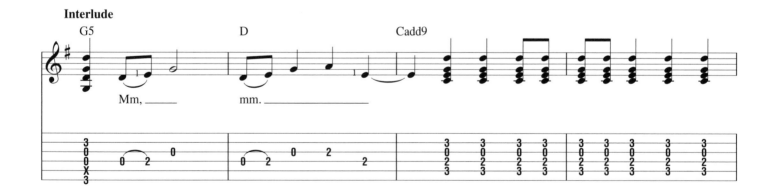

Mm, ___ mm. ___

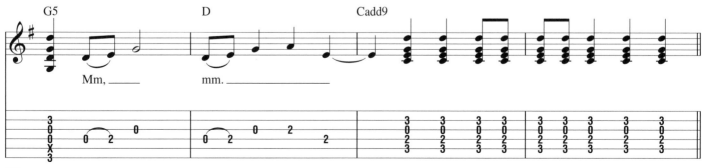

Mm, ___ mm. ___

**Verse**

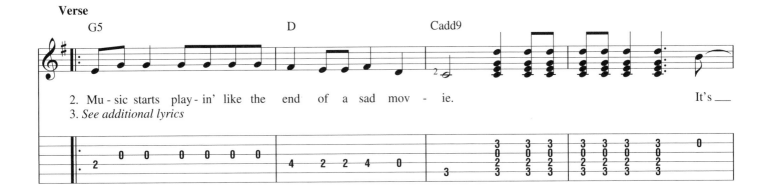

2. Mu - sic starts play - in' like the end of a sad mov - ie. It's ___
3. *See additional lyrics*

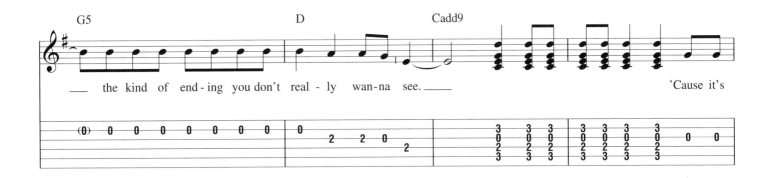

___ the kind of end - ing you don't real - ly wan - na see. ___ 'Cause it's

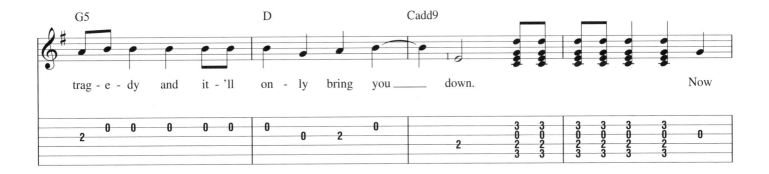

trag - e - dy and it - 'll on - ly bring you ___ down. Now

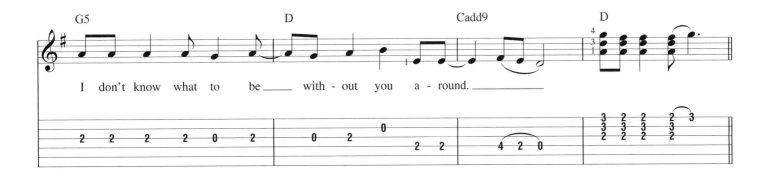

I don't know what to be ___ with - out you a - round. ___

**Pre-Chorus**

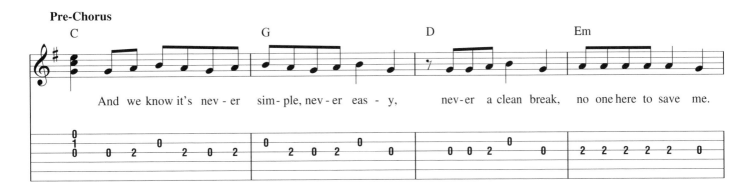

And we know it's nev - er sim - ple, nev - er eas - y, nev - er a clean break, no one here to save me.

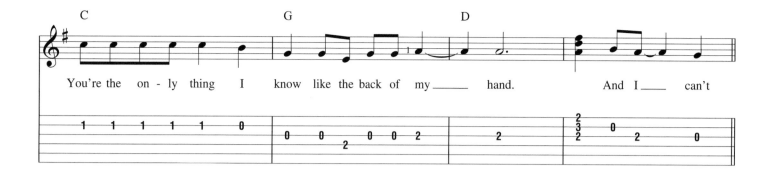

You're the on-ly thing I know like the back of my _____ hand. And I _____ can't

**Chorus**

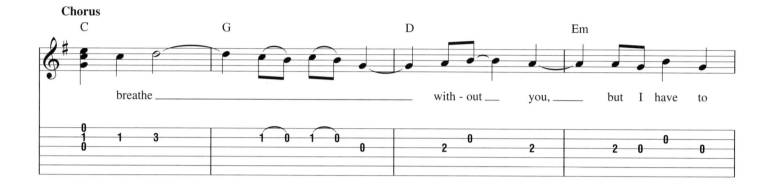

breathe _____ with-out _____ you, _____ but I have to

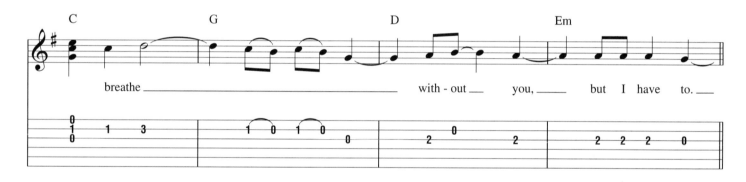

breathe _____ with-out _____ you, _____ but I have to. _____

1.

**Interlude**

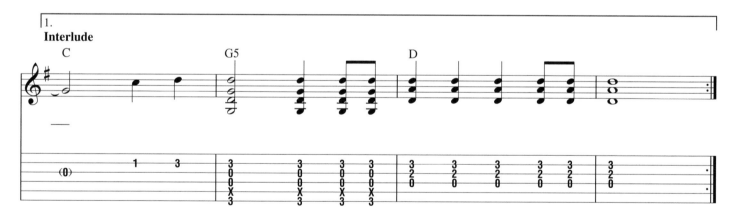

2.

**Interlude**

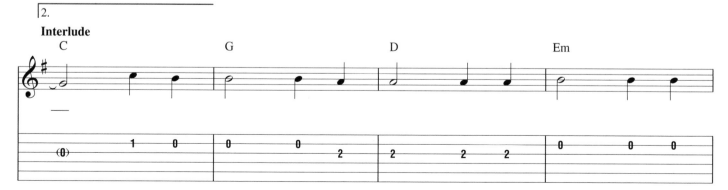

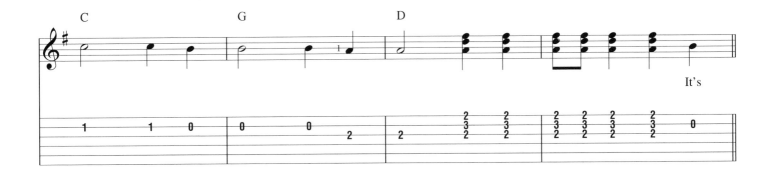

**Bridge**

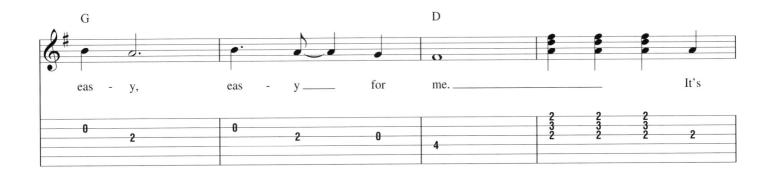

two A. - M.,____ feel-in' like I just lost a ____ friend.____ Hope you know this ain't

eas - y, eas - y ____ for me. _____ It's

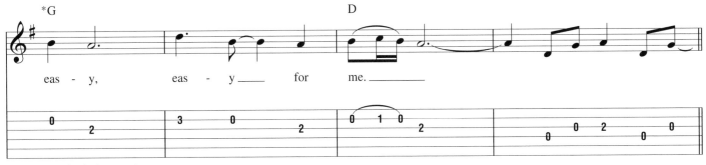

two A. - M. ____ feel-in' like I just lost a ____ friend. ____ Hope you know this ain't

eas - y, eas - y ____ for me. ____

*Let chords ring next 4 meas.

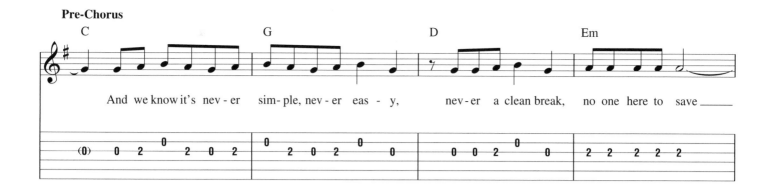

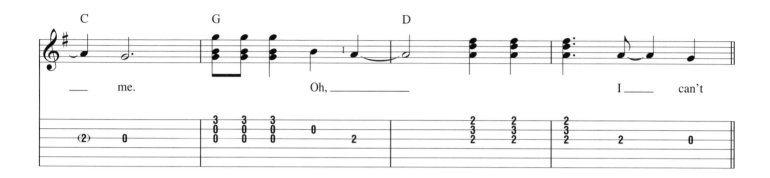

**Chorus**

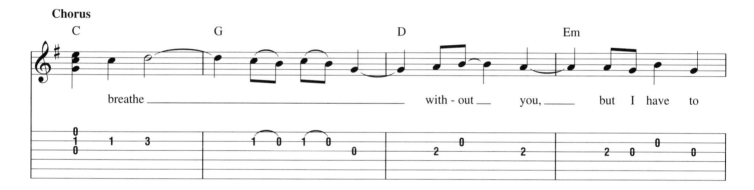

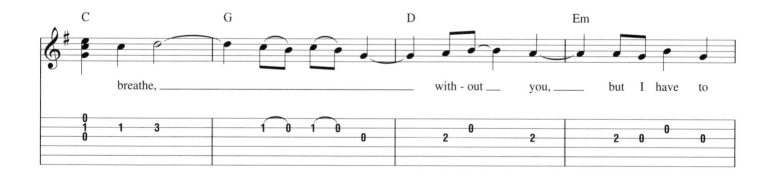

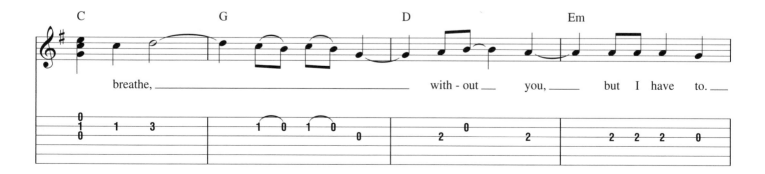

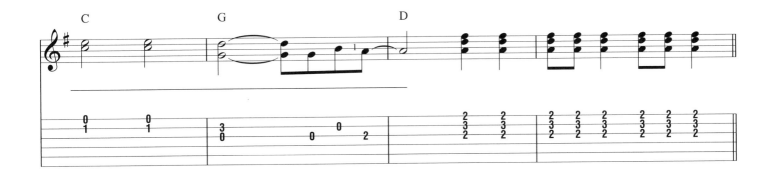

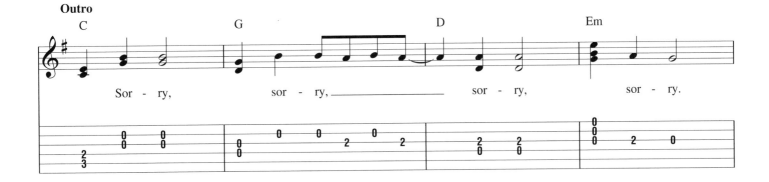

**Outro**

Sor - ry, sor - ry, _____ sor - ry, sor - ry.

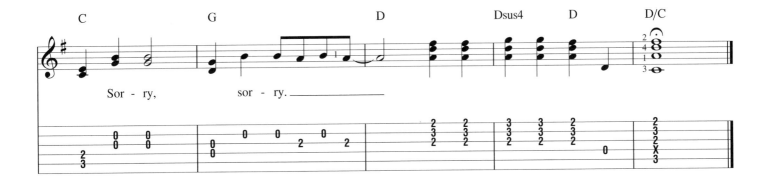

Sor - ry, sor - ry. _____

*Additional Lyrics*

3. Never wanted this, never want to see you hurt.
   Ev'ry little bump in the road, I tried to swerve.
   People are people and sometimes it doesn't work out.
   Nothin' we say is gonna save us from the fallout.

# Tell Me Why

### Words and Music by Taylor Swift and Liz Rose

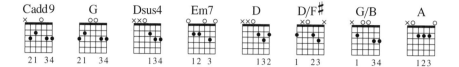

**Strum Pattern: 2, 4**
**Pick Pattern: 6**

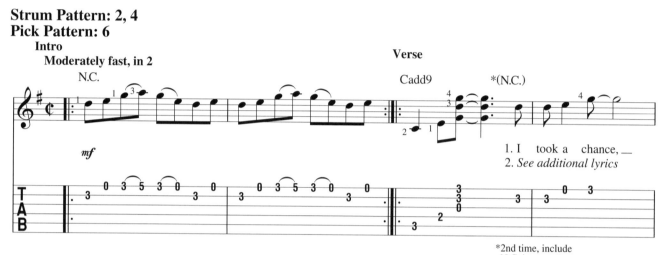

1. I took a chance, __
2. *See additional lyrics*

*2nd time, include
N.C. in parentheses.

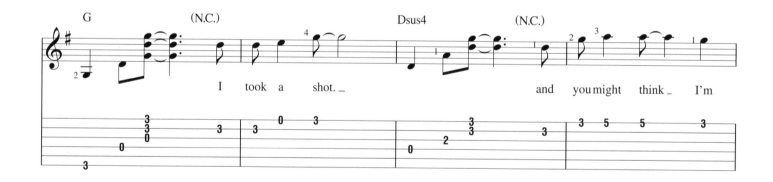

I took a shot. __ and you might think __ I'm

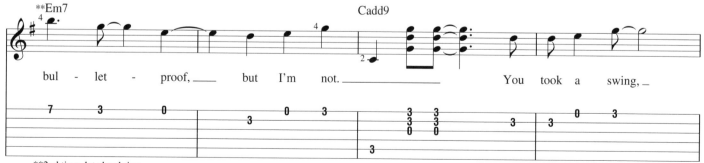

bul - let - proof, __ but I'm not. __ You took a swing, __

**2nd time, let chord ring.

**Chorus**

*Sung one octave higher throughout Chorus.

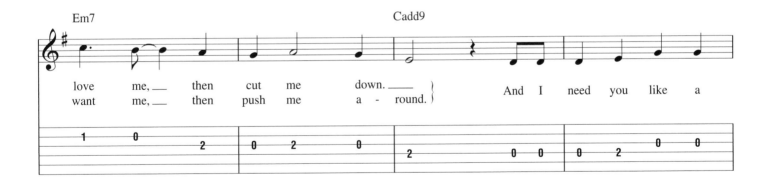

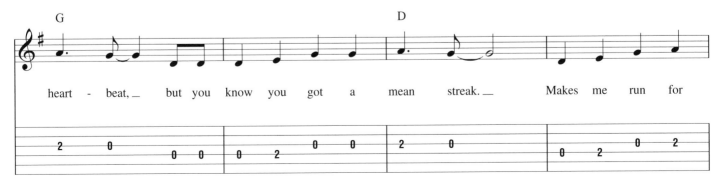

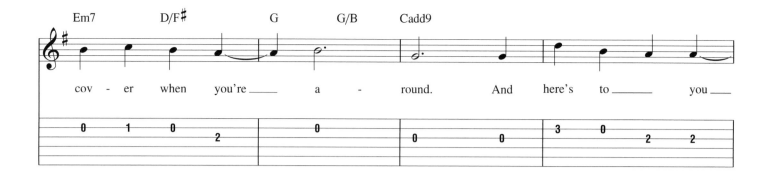

cov - er when you're _____ a - round. And here's to _____ you _____

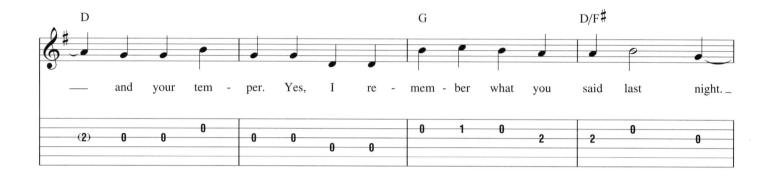

_____ and your tem - per. Yes, I re - mem - ber what you said last night. _

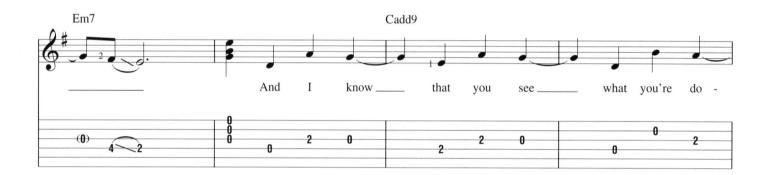

_____ And I know _____ that you see _____ what you're do -

1.
w/ Intro riff

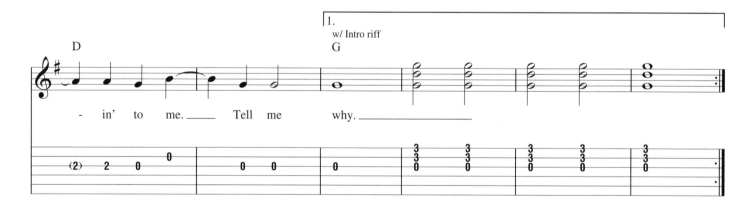

- in' to me. _____ Tell me why. _____

2.

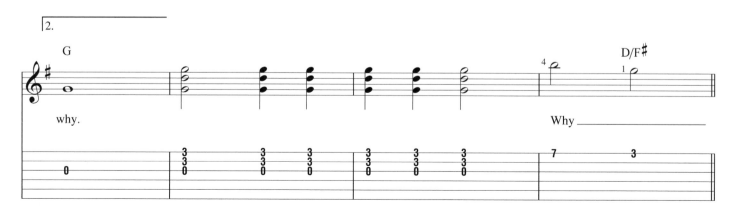

why. Why _____

**Bridge**

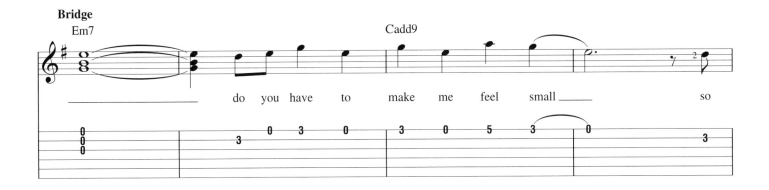

do you have to make me feel small _____ so

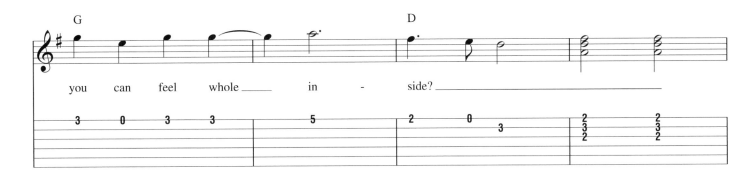

you can feel whole _____ in - side? _____

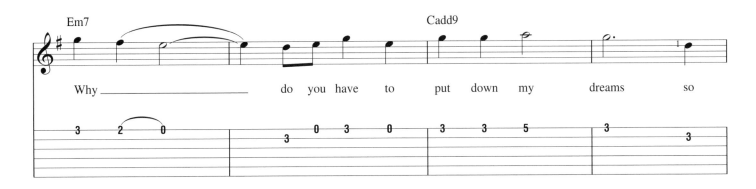

Why _____ do you have to put down my dreams so

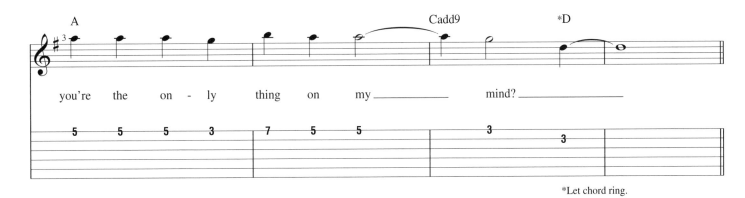

you're the on - ly thing on my _____ mind? _____

*Let chord ring.

**Chorus**

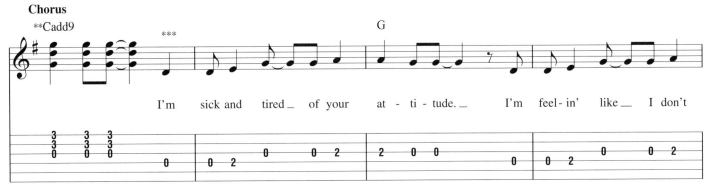

I'm sick and tired __ of your at - ti - tude. __ I'm feel-in' like __ I don't

**Let chords ring, next 8 meas.
***Sung one octave higher throughout Chorus.

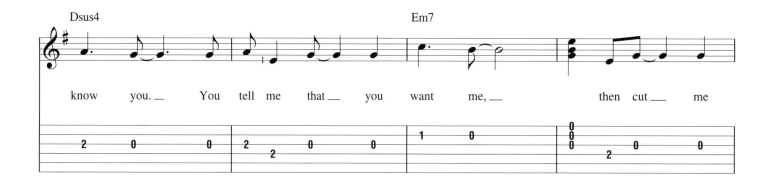

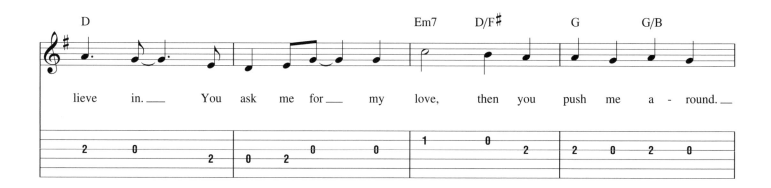

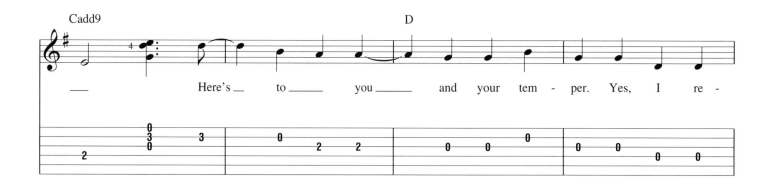

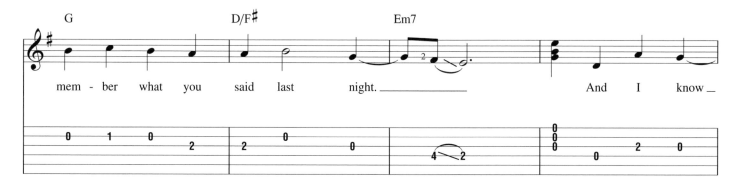

**Outro**
w/ Intro riff

*Sung as written.

### Additional Lyrics

2. You could write a book on how
To ruin someone's perfect day.
Well, I get so confused and frustrated,
Forget what I'm tryin' to say. Oh…

# You're Not Sorry

**Words and Music by Taylor Swift**

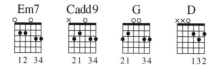

*Tune down 1/2 step:
(low to high) Eb-Ab-Db-Gb-Bb-Eb

**Strum Pattern: 5**
**Pick Pattern: 1**

**Intro**
**Moderately slow, in 2**

*Optional: To match recording, tune down 1/2 step.

**Verse**

1. All this time I was wast-in', hop-in' you would come a-round. I've been
2. *See additional lyrics*

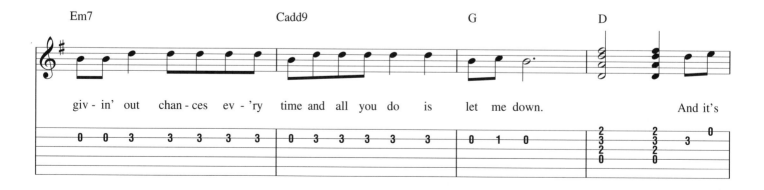

giv-in' out chan-ces ev-'ry time and all you do is let me down. And it's

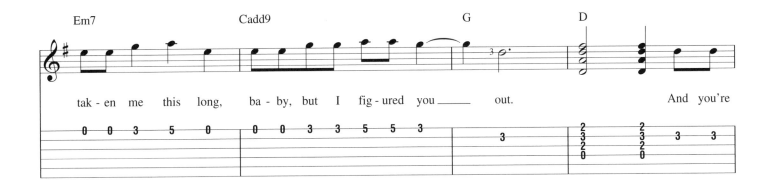

tak - en me this long, ba - by, but I fig - ured you _____ out. And you're

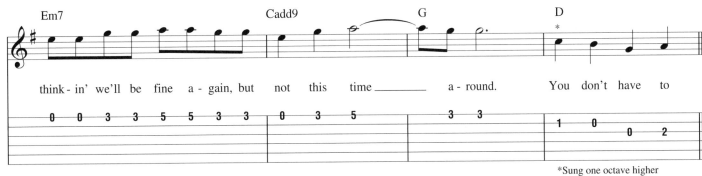

think - in' we'll be fine a - gain, but not this time _____ a - round. You don't have to

*Sung one octave higher
 throughout Chorus.

## 𝄋 Chorus

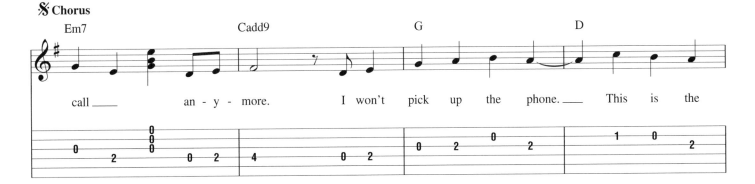

call _____ an - y - more. I won't pick up the phone. _____ This is the

last _____ straw.

{ 1., 2. Don't wan - na hurt an - y - more. _____ }
{ 3. There's noth - in' left to beg for. _____ } And you can

tell me that you're sor - ry, but I don't be - lieve you, ba - by, like I did be - fore. _____

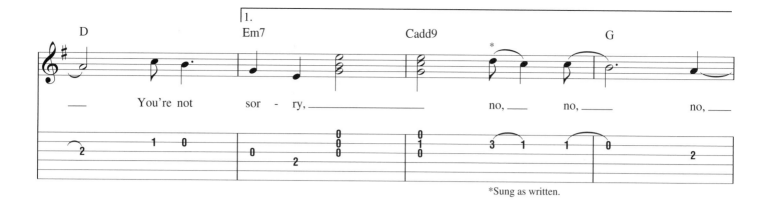

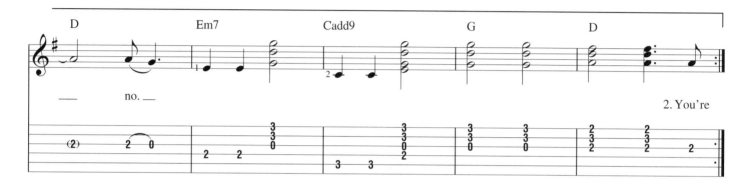

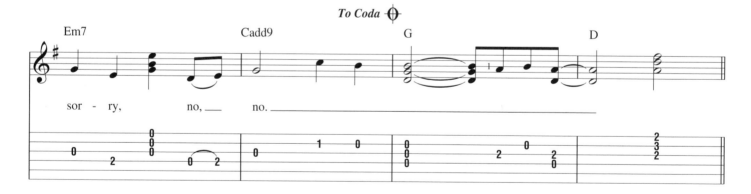

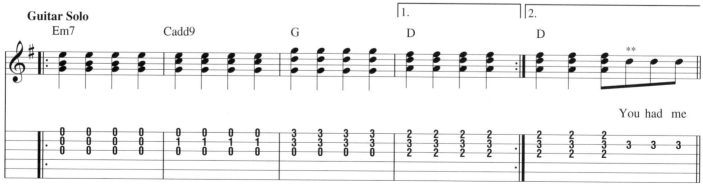

*Sung one octave higher till end.

You're not...

*rit.*

### Additional Lyrics

3. You're lookin' so innocent I might
   Believe you if I didn't know.
   Could've loved you all my life if you hadn't
   Left me waitin' in the cold.
   And you got your share of secrets and
   I'm tired of bein' last to know.
   And now you're askin' me to listen 'cause
   It's worked each time before.
   But you don't have to...

# The Way I Loved You

### Words and Music by Taylor Swift and John Rich

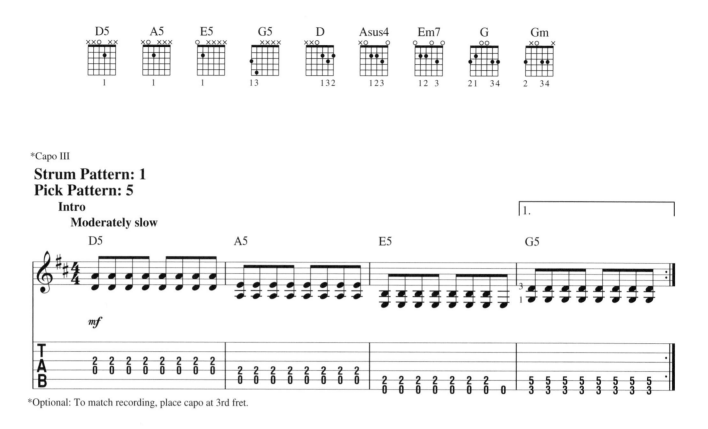

*Capo III

**Strum Pattern: 1**
**Pick Pattern: 5**

Intro

Moderately slow

*Optional: To match recording, place capo at 3rd fret.

1. He is sens - i - ble _ and so in - cred - i - ble _ and

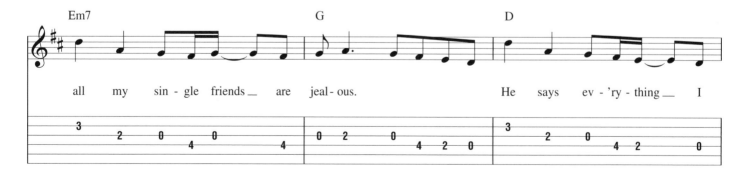

all my sin - gle friends _ are jeal - ous. He says ev - 'ry - thing _ I

*Let chord ring.

## 𝄋 Chorus

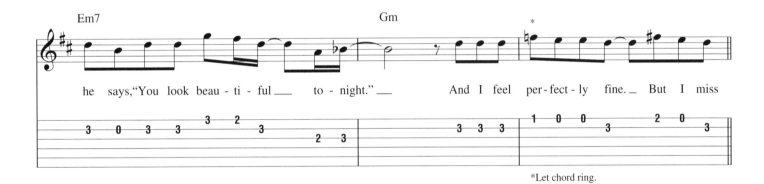

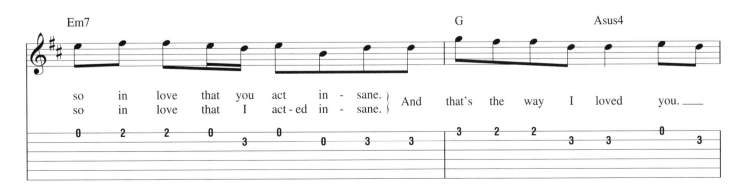

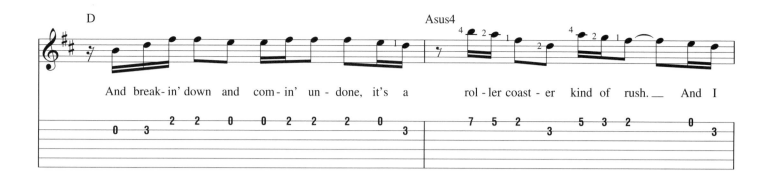

And break-in' down and com-in' un-done, it's a roll-er coast-er kind of rush. __ And I

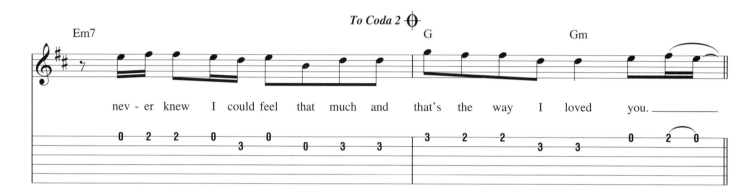

*To Coda 2*

nev-er knew I could feel that much and that's the way I loved you. _____

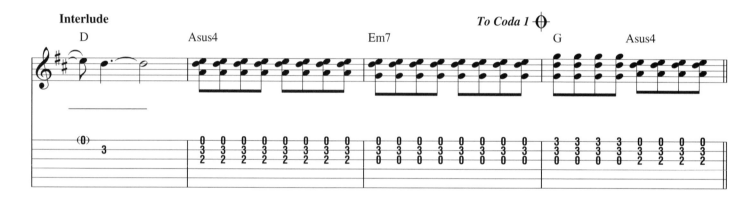

**Interlude**

*To Coda 1*

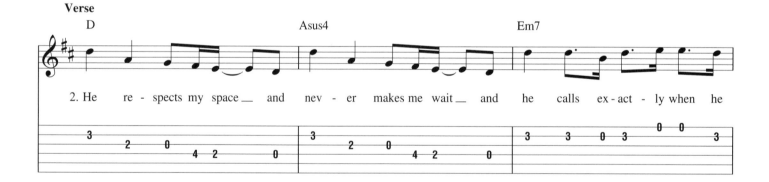

**Verse**

2. He re-spects my space __ and nev-er makes me wait __ and he calls ex-act-ly when he

says he will. _____ He's close to my moth-er, talks bus-'ness with my fath-er. He's

*Let chord ring.

**Coda 1**

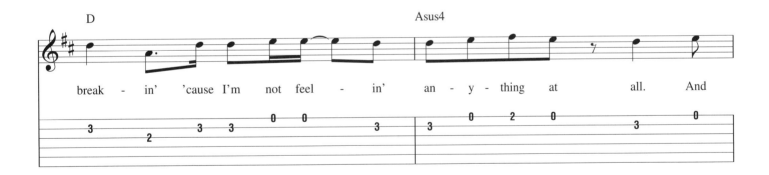

Asus4                                *G

Got a - way ___ by some ___ mis - take ___ and now.       I miss

*Let chord ring.

## ⊕ Coda 2

**Outro**
w/ Voc. ad lib.

G         Asus4         D              Asus4

that's the way I loved you. ___

Em7             G     Asus4      D         Asus4

And that's the way I loved you. __

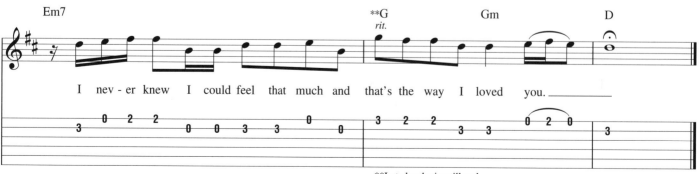

Em7                            **G        Gm        D
                                    *rit.*

I nev - er knew I could feel that much and that's the way I loved you. ___

**Let chords ring till end.

58

# Forever & Always

**Words and Music by Taylor Swift**

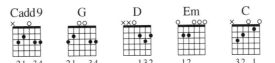

*Capo III

**Strum Pattern: 1**
**Pick Pattern: 5**

**Verse**
**Moderately fast**

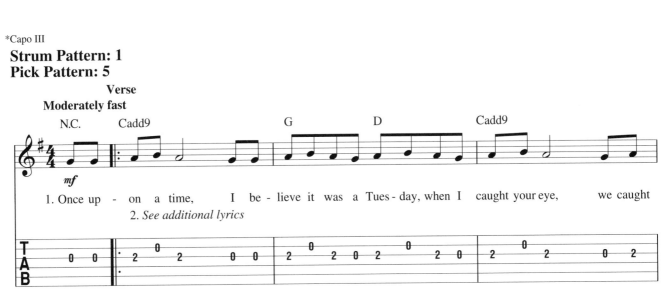

1. Once up - on a time, I be - lieve it was a Tues - day, when I caught your eye, we caught
2. *See additional lyrics*

*Optional: To match recording, place capo at 3rd fret.

on to some - thin'. I hold on - to the night you looked me in the eye and told me you loved me. __

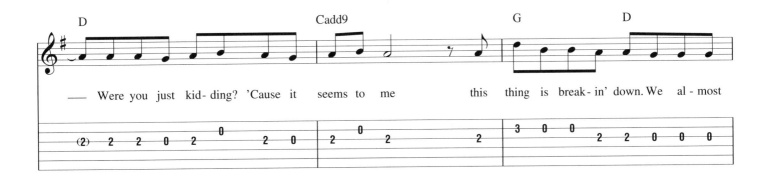

__ Were you just kid - ding? 'Cause it seems to me this thing is break - in' down. We al - most

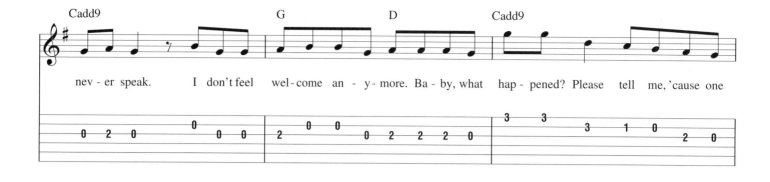

nev - er speak. I don't feel wel-come an - y - more. Ba - by, what hap - pened? Please tell me, 'cause one

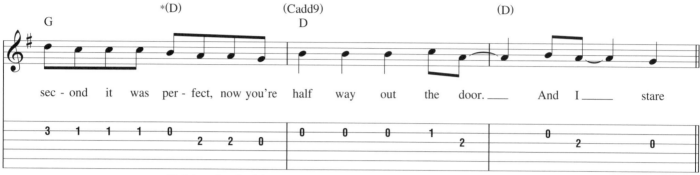

sec - ond it was per - fect, now you're half way out the door.___ And I ___ stare

*2nd time, play chords in parens.

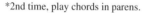

**Pre-Chorus**

at the phone.__ He still has-n't called__ and then you feel so low, you can't feel noth - in' at all.__ And you

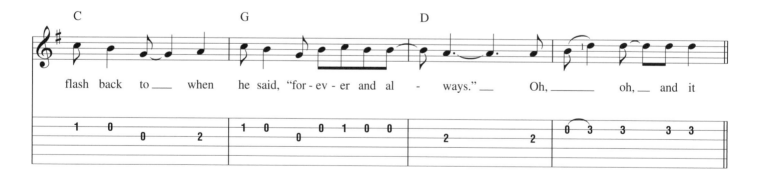

flash back to ___ when he said, "for - ev - er and al - ways."___ Oh, _____ oh, __ and it

**%Chorus**

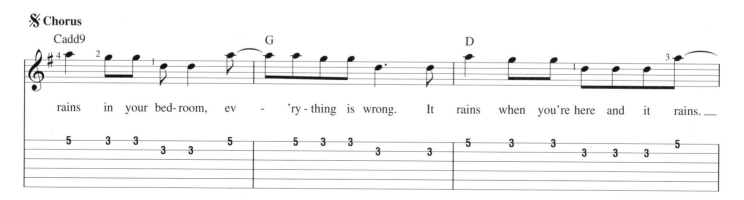

rains in your bed-room, ev - 'ry - thing is wrong. It rains when you're here and it rains.__

*Let chord ring.

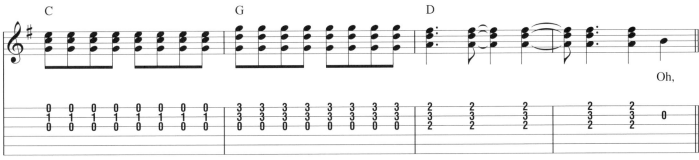

**Bridge**

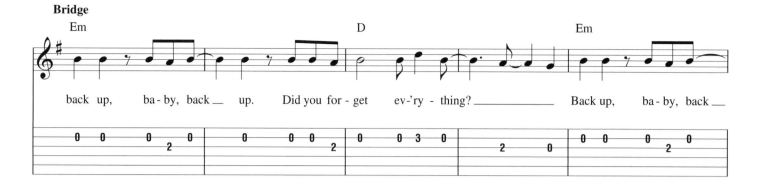

back up, ba-by, back __ up. Did you for-get ev-'ry-thing? _____ Back up, ba-by, back __

*D.S. al Coda*

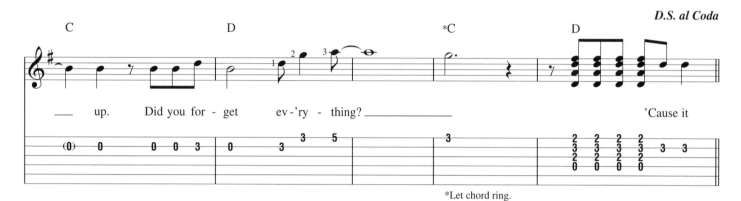

__ up. Did you for-get ev-'ry-thing? _____ 'Cause it

*Let chord ring.

⊕ **Coda**

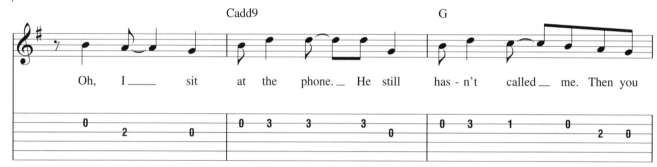

Oh, I __ sit at the phone. __ He still has-n't called __ me. Then you

feel so low, you can't feel __ noth-in' at all. __ And you flash back to __ when we __ said, "for-ev-er and al-

**Outro-Chorus**

-ways." _____ And it rains in your bed-room, ev-'ry-thing is wrong. It

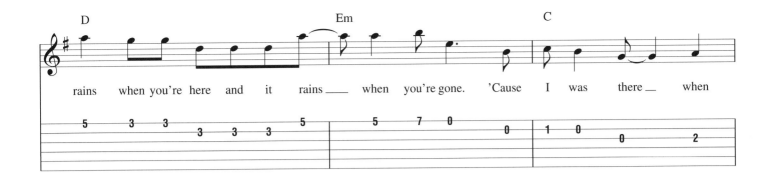

rains     when you're here     and     it     rains ____ when     you're gone.     'Cause     I     was     there ____ when

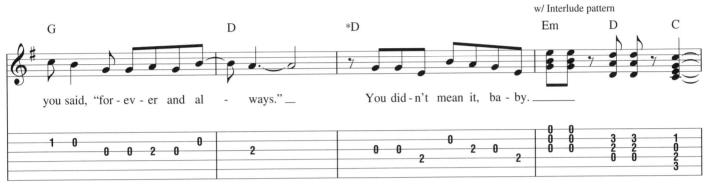

you said, "for - ev - er  and  al  -  ways." ___          You did - n't  mean  it,  ba - by. _____

*Let chord ring.

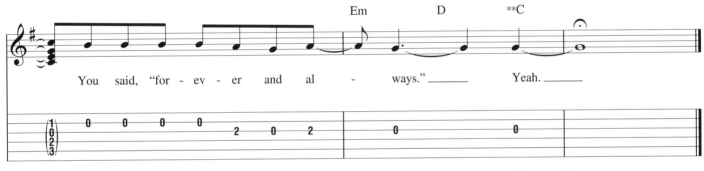

You  said, "for - ev - er  and  al  -  ways." _____  Yeah. _____

**Let chord ring.

*Additional Lyrics*

2. Was I out of line? Did I say somethin' way too honest?
   Made you run and hide like a scared little boy.
   I looked into your eyes. Thought I knew you for a minute.
   Now I'm not so sure.
   So, here's ev'rything coming down to nothin'.
   Here's to silence that cuts me to the core.
   Where is this going? Thought I knew for a minute,
   But I don't anymore.

# The Best Day

**Words and Music by Taylor Swift**

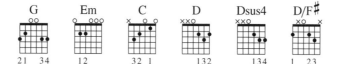

*Capo VI

**Strum Pattern: 4, 6**
**Pick Pattern: 4, 5**

Intro
Moderately

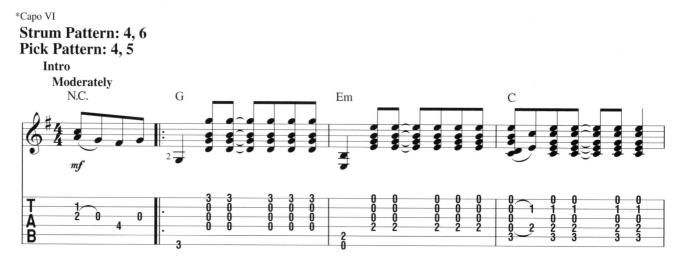

*Optional: To match recording, place capo at 6th fret.

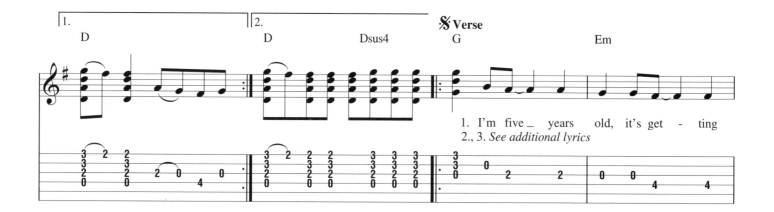

1. I'm five _ years old, it's get - ting
2., 3. *See additional lyrics*

cold, I've got _ my big coat on. _ I hear _ you laugh and look _ up,

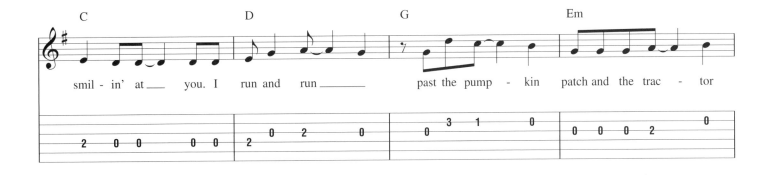

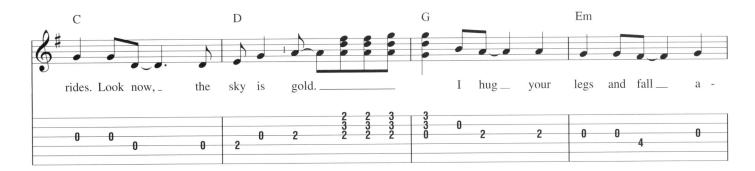

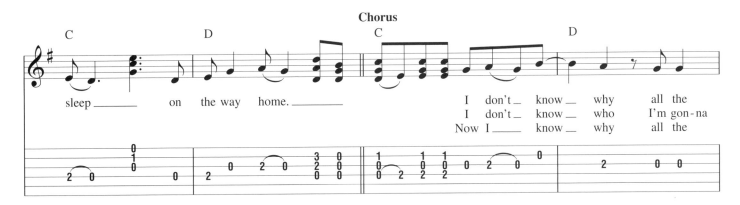

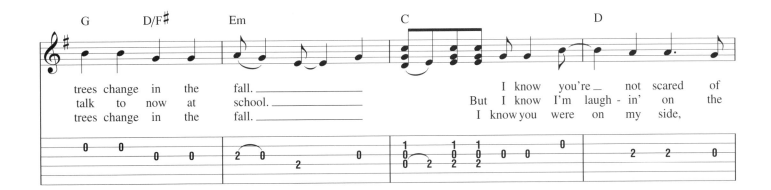

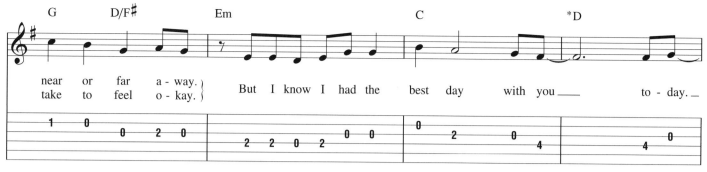

near or far a - way. }
take to feel o - kay. }
But I know I had the best day with you _____ to - day. _____

*Let chord ring.

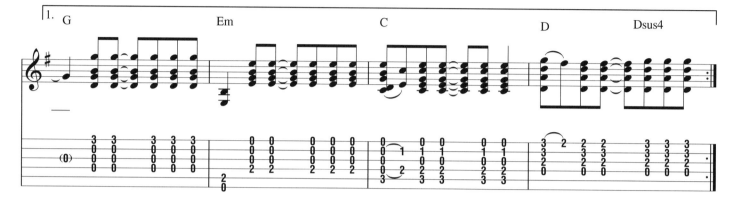

1. G          Em          C          D          Dsus4

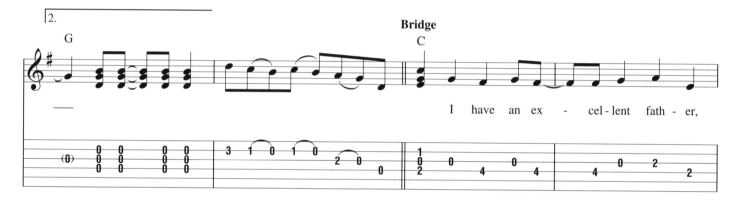

2.
G                              Bridge
                               C

I have an ex - cel - lent fath - er,

Em                                        C

his strength is mak - in' me strong - er.          God smiles on my _____ lit - tle broth - er.

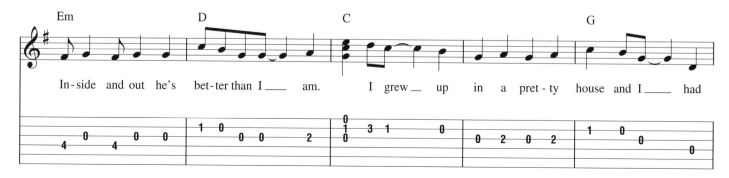

Em          D          C          G

In - side and out he's bet - ter than I _____ am.          I grew _____ up in a pret - ty house and I _____ had

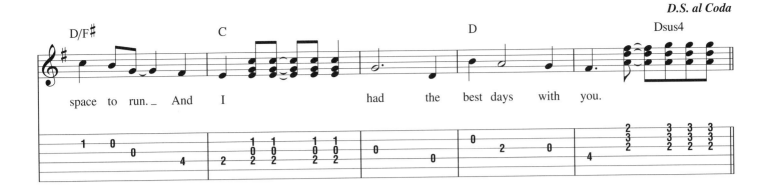

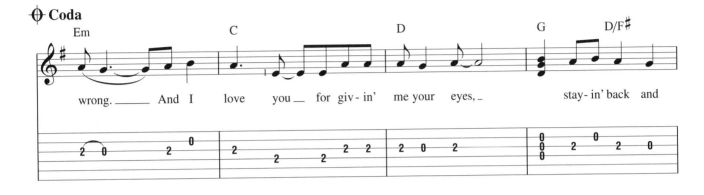

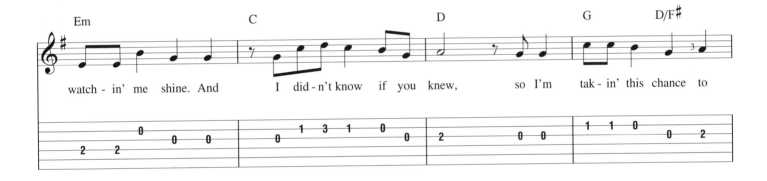

*Additional Lyrics*

2. I'm thirteen now and don't know my friends could be so mean.
   I come home cryin' and you hold me tight and grab the keys.
   And we drive and drive until we found a town far enough away.
   And we talk and window shop till I've forgotten all their names.

3. There is a video I found from back when I was three.
   You set up a paint set in the kitchen and you're talkin' to me.
   It's the age of princesses and pirate ships and seven dwarfs.
   And daddy's smart and you're the prettiest lady in the whole wide world.

# Change

**Words and Music by Taylor Swift**

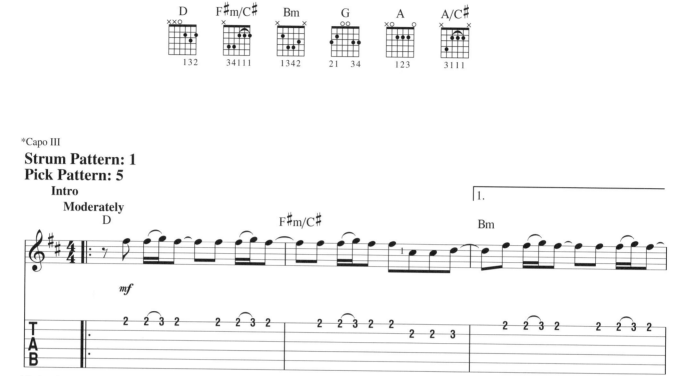

*Capo III

**Strum Pattern: 1**
**Pick Pattern: 5**

*Optional: To match recording, place capo at 3rd fret.

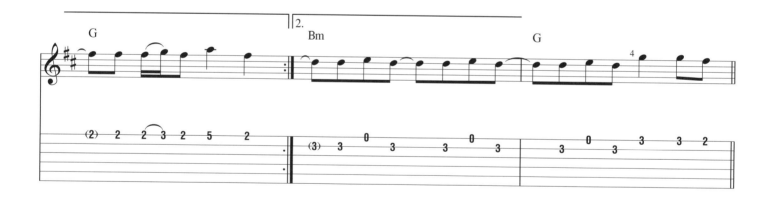

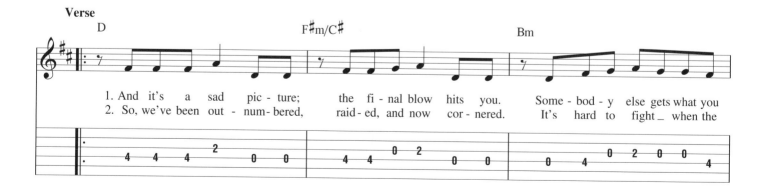

1. And it's a sad pic-ture; the fi-nal blow hits you. Some-bod-y else gets what you
2. So, we've been out-num-bered, raid-ed, and now cor-nered. It's hard to fight _ when the

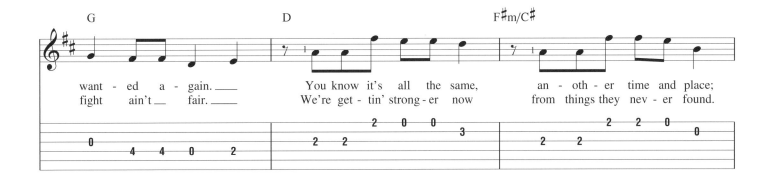

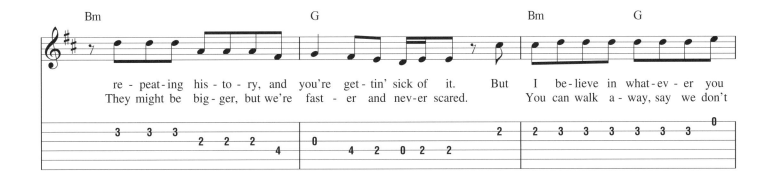

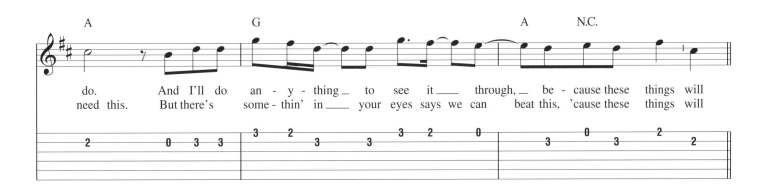

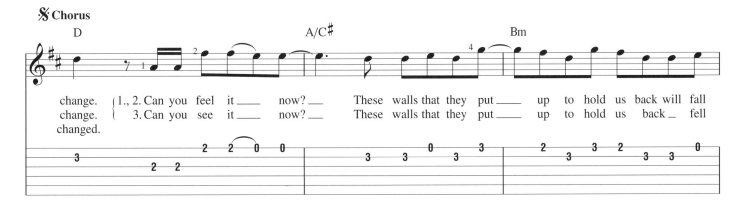

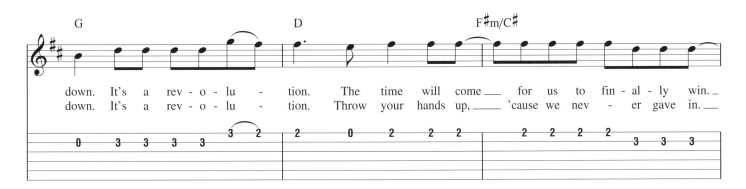

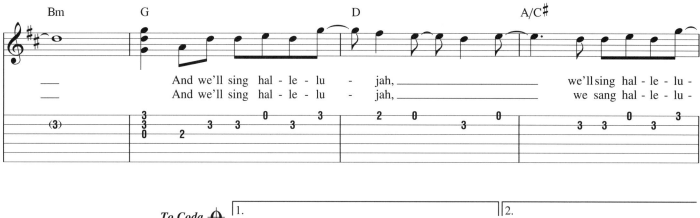

And we'll sing hal - le - lu - jah, _____ we'll sing hal - le - lu -
And we'll sing hal - le - lu - jah, _____ we sang hal - le - lu -

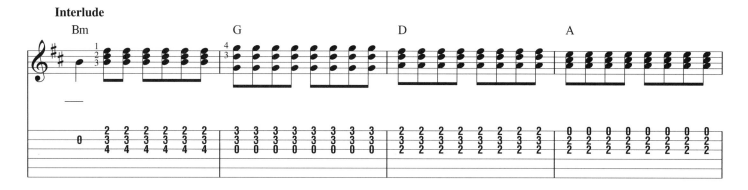

*To Coda* ⊕

- jah, _____ oh, _____ oh. _____ oh, _____ oh. _____
- jah, _____

*Let chord ring.

**Interlude**

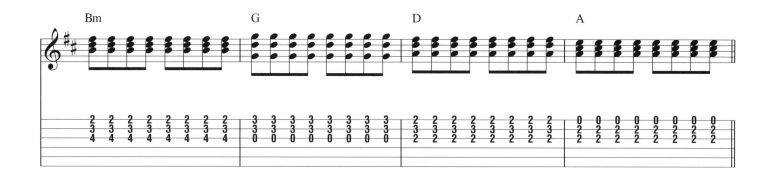

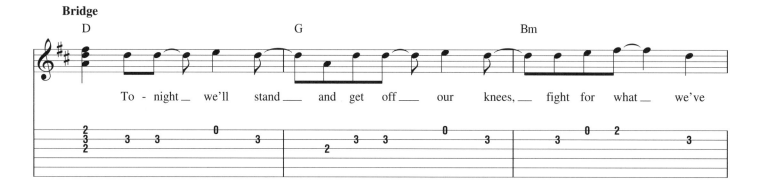

**Bridge**

To - night __ we'll stand __ and get off __ our knees, __ fight for what __ we've

worked for ___ all ___ these years. And the bat-tle was long. ___ It's the fight ___ of our lives, ___

D.S. al Coda

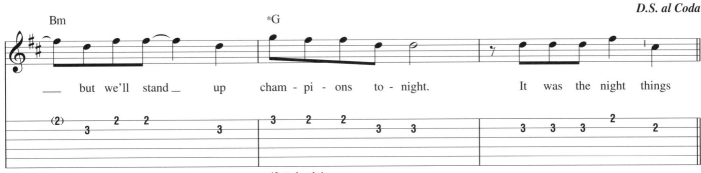

___ but we'll stand ___ up cham-pi-ons to-night. It was the night things

*Let chord ring.

**Coda**

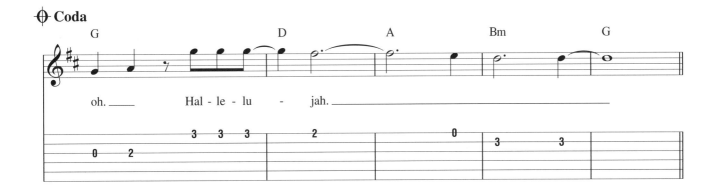

oh. ___ Hal-le-lu - jah. ___

**Outro**

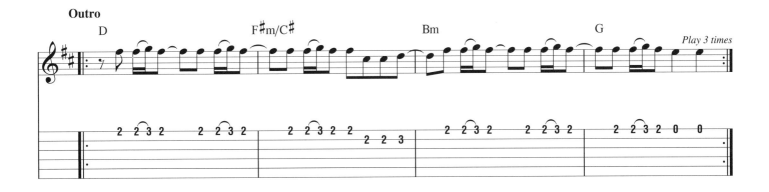

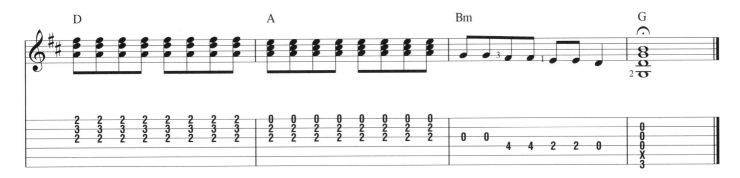

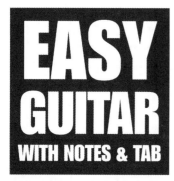

# EASY GUITAR
## WITH NOTES & TAB

*This series features simplified arrangements with notes, tab, chord charts, and strum and pick patterns.*

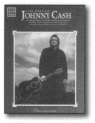

## MIXED FOLIOS

| | | |
|---|---|---|
| 00702002 | Acoustic Rock Hits for Easy Guitar | $12.95 |
| 00702166 | All-Time Best Guitar Collection | $17.95 |
| 00699665 | Beatles Best | $12.95 |
| 00702232 | Best Acoustic Songs for Easy Guitar | $12.99 |
| 00702233 | Best Hard Rock Songs | $14.99 |
| 00698978 | Big Christmas Collection | $16.95 |
| 00702115 | Blues Classics | $10.95 |
| 00385020 | Broadway Songs for Kids | $9.95 |
| 00702237 | Christian Acoustic Favorites | $12.95 |
| 00702149 | Children's Christian Songbook | $7.95 |
| 00702028 | Christmas Classics | $7.95 |
| 00702185 | Christmas Hits | $9.95 |
| 00702016 | Classic Blues for Easy Guitar | $12.95 |
| 00702141 | Classic Rock | $8.95 |
| 00702203 | CMT's 100 Greatest Country Songs | $27.95 |
| 00702170 | Contemporary Christian Christmas | $9.95 |
| 00702006 | Contemporary Christian Favorites | $9.95 |
| 00702065 | Contemporary Women of Country | $9.95 |
| 00702121 | Country from the Heart | $9.95 |
| 00702240 | Country Hits of 2007-2008 | $12.95 |
| 00702225 | Country Hits of '06-'07 | $12.95 |
| 00702085 | Disney Movie Hits | $12.95 |
| 00702257 | Easy Acoustic Guitar Songs | $14.99 |
| 00702212 | Essential Christmas | $9.95 |
| 00702041 | Favorite Hymns for Easy Guitar | $9.95 |
| 00702174 | God Bless America® & Other Songs for a Better Nation | $8.95 |
| 00699374 | Gospel Favorites | $14.95 |
| 00702160 | The Great American Country Songbook | $12.95 |
| 00702050 | Great Classical Themes for Easy Guitar | $6.95 |
| 00702131 | Great Country Hits of the '90s | $8.95 |
| 00702116 | Greatest Hymns for Guitar | $8.95 |
| 00702130 | The Groovy Years | $9.95 |
| 00702184 | Guitar Instrumentals | $9.95 |
| 00702231 | High School Musical for Easy Guitar | $12.95 |
| 00702241 | High School Musical 2 | $12.95 |
| 00702249 | High School Musical 3 | $12.99 |
| 00702037 | Hits of the '50s for Easy Guitar | $10.95 |
| 00702046 | Hits of the '70s for Easy Guitar | $8.95 |
| 00702047 | Hits of the '80s for Easy Guitar | $9.95 |
| 00702032 | International Songs for Easy Guitar | $12.95 |
| 00702051 | Jock Rock for Easy Guitar | $9.95 |
| 00702162 | Jumbo Easy Guitar Songbook | $19.95 |
| 00702112 | Latin Favorites | $9.95 |
| 00702258 | Legends of Rock | $14.99 |
| 00702138 | Mellow Rock Hits | $10.95 |
| 00702147 | Motown's Greatest Hits | $9.95 |
| 00702114 | Movie Love Songs | $9.95 |
| 00702039 | Movie Themes | $10.95 |
| 00702210 | Best of MTV Unplugged | $12.95 |
| 00702189 | MTV's 100 Greatest Pop Songs | $24.95 |
| 00702187 | Selections from *O Brother Where Art Thou?* | $12.95 |
| 00702178 | 100 Songs for Kids | $12.95 |
| 00702158 | Songs from Passion | $9.95 |
| 00702125 | Praise and Worship for Guitar | $9.95 |
| 00702155 | Rock Hits for Guitar | $9.95 |
| 00702242 | Rock Band | $19.95 |
| 00702256 | Rock Band 2 | $19.99 |
| 00702128 | Rockin' Down the Highway | $9.95 |
| 00702207 | Smash Hits for Guitar | $9.95 |
| 00702110 | The Sound of Music | $9.99 |
| 00702124 | Today's Christian Rock – 2nd Edition | $9.95 |
| 00702220 | Today's Country Hits | $9.95 |
| 00702198 | Today's Hits for Guitar | $9.95 |
| 00702217 | Top Christian Hits | $12.95 |
| 00702235 | Top Christian Hits of '07-'08 | $14.95 |
| 00702246 | Top Hits of 2008 | $12.95 |
| 00702206 | Very Best of Rock | $9.95 |
| 00702175 | VH1's 100 Greatest Songs of Rock and Roll | $24.95 |
| 00702192 | Worship Favorites | $9.95 |

## ARTIST COLLECTIONS

| | | |
|---|---|---|
| 00702001 | Best of Aerosmith | $16.95 |
| 00702040 | Best of the Allman Brothers | $12.95 |
| 00702169 | Best of The Beach Boys | $10.95 |
| 00702201 | The Essential Black Sabbath | $12.95 |
| 00702140 | Best of Brooks & Dunn | $10.95 |
| 00702095 | Best of Mariah Carey | $12.95 |
| 00702043 | Best of Johnny Cash | $12.95 |
| 00702033 | Best of Steven Curtis Chapman | $14.95 |
| 00702073 | Steven Curtis Chapman – Favorites | $10.95 |
| 00702090 | Eric Clapton's Best | $10.95 |
| 00702086 | Eric Clapton – from the Album *Unplugged* | $10.95 |
| 00702202 | The Essential Eric Clapton | $12.95 |
| 00702250 | blink-182 – Greatest Hits | $12.99 |
| 00702053 | Best of Patsy Cline | $10.95 |
| 00702229 | The Very Best of Creedence Clearwater Revival | $12.95 |
| 00702145 | Best of Jim Croce | $10.95 |
| 00702219 | David Crowder*Band Collection | $12.95 |
| 00702122 | The Doors for Easy Guitar | $12.99 |
| 00702099 | Best of Amy Grant | $9.95 |
| 00702190 | Best of Pat Green | $19.95 |
| 00702136 | Best of Merle Haggard | $10.95 |
| 00702243 | Hannah Montana | $14.95 |
| 00702244 | Hannah Montana 2/Meet Miley Cyrus | $16.95 |
| 00702227 | Jimi Hendrix – Smash Hits | $14.99 |
| 00702236 | Best of Antonio Carlos Jobim | $12.95 |
| 00702087 | Best of Billy Joel | $10.95 |
| 00702245 | Elton John – Greatest Hits 1970-2002 | $14.99 |
| 00702204 | Robert Johnson | $9.95 |
| 00702199 | Norah Jones – Come Away with Me | $10.95 |
| 00702234 | Selections from Toby Keith – 35 Biggest Hits | $12.95 |
| 00702003 | Kiss | $9.95 |
| 00702193 | Best of Jennifer Knapp | $12.95 |
| 00702097 | John Lennon – Imagine | $9.95 |
| 00702216 | Lynyrd Skynyrd | $14.95 |
| 00702182 | The Essential Bob Marley | $12.95 |
| 00702129 | Songs of Sarah McLachlan | $12.95 |
| 02501316 | Metallica – Death Magnetic | $15.95 |
| 00702209 | Steve Miller Band – Young Hearts (Greatest Hits) | $12.95 |
| 00702096 | Best of Nirvana | $14.95 |
| 00702211 | The Offspring – Greatest Hits | $12.95 |
| 00702030 | Best of Roy Orbison | $12.95 |
| 00702144 | Best of Ozzy Osbourne | $12.95 |
| 00702139 | Elvis Country Favorites | $9.95 |
| 00699415 | Best of Queen for Guitar | $14.99 |
| 00702208 | Red Hot Chili Peppers – Greatest Hits | $12.95 |
| 00702093 | Rolling Stones Collection | $17.95 |
| 00702092 | Best of the Rolling Stones | $14.99 |
| 00702196 | Best of Bob Seger | $12.95 |
| 00702252 | Frank Sinatra – Nothing But the Best | $12.99 |
| 00702010 | Best of Rod Stewart | $14.95 |
| 00702150 | Best of Sting | $12.95 |
| 00702049 | Best of George Strait | $12.95 |
| 00702259 | Taylor Swift for Easy Guitar | $12.99 |
| 00702223 | Chris Tomlin – Arriving | $12.95 |
| 00702226 | Chris Tomlin – See the Morning | $12.95 |
| 00702132 | Shania Twain – Greatest Hits | $10.95 |
| 00702108 | Best of Stevie Ray Vaughan | $10.95 |
| 00702123 | Best of Hank Williams | $9.95 |
| 00702111 | Stevie Wonder – Guitar Collection | $9.95 |
| 00702228 | Neil Young – Greatest Hits | $12.99 |
| 00702188 | Essential ZZ Top | $10.95 |

Prices, contents and availability subject to change without notice.

FOR MORE INFORMATION, SEE YOUR LOCAL MUSIC DEALER, OR WRITE TO:

HAL•LEONARD® CORPORATION

7777 W. BLUEMOUND RD. P.O. BOX 13819 MILWAUKEE, WI 53213

Visit Hal Leonard online at **www.halleonard.com**

0709